THINGS TO COME
FOR PLANET EARTH

What the <u>Bible</u> Says About the Last Times

Aaron Luther Plueger

Publishing House
St. Louis

Concordia Publishing House, St. Louis, Missouri
Copyright © 1977 Concordia Publishing House

Manufactured in the United States of America

Library of Congress Cataloging in Publication Data

Plueger, Aaron L 1926-
    Things to come for planet Earth.

    Includes bibliographical references.
    1. Eschatology—Biblical teaching. 2. Bible—Prophecies. I. Title.
BS680.E8P58   236   77-23598
ISBN 0-570-03762-X

Contents

Quotations from

Grier, W. J., *Momentous Event*. The Banner of Truth Trust, London, 1945;

Holman Study Bible—Revised Standard Version. A. J. Holman Co., Philadelphia, 1962;

Lindsey, Hal and C. C. Carlson, *The Late Great Planet Earth*. Zondervan Publishing House, Grand Rapids, Mich., 1970;

Lowry, Cecil John, *Christian Catechism*. Color Art Press, Oakland, Calif., 1961;

Murray, George L., *Millennial Studies: A Search for Truth*. Baker Book House, Grand Rapids, Mich., 1948;

New American Standard Bible. The Lockman Foundation, La Habra, Calif., and A. J. Holman Co., Philadelphia, 1975;

Pentecost, J. Dwight, *Things to Come*. Dunham Publishing Co., Findlay, Ohio, 1958; reprinted by Zondervan Publishing House, Grand Rapids, Mich.;

Spurgeon, C. H., *The Treasury of the Bible*. Zondervan Publishing House, Grand Rapids, Mich., 1962;

Thomas, L. R., *Does the Bible Teach Millennialism?* Reiner Publications, Swengel, Pa., n. d.;

Young, Edward J., *The Prophecy of Daniel*. Wm. B. Eerdmans Publishing Co., Grand Rapids, Mich., 1949

are used by permission of the publishers.

List of Abbreviations

KJV: King James Version
LXX: Septuagint
NASB: New American Standard Bible
RSV: Revised Standard Version
WFB: An American Translation by William F. Beck

List of Charts

Introduction

These are perilous times for the soul. Yet in these last days God has spoken to us by His Son, who points out dangers, not the least of which is that of being deceived about things to come. Even the elect are alerted against being misled about Christ's return.

This is how things stand in the last quarter of the 20th century. On the one hand, Bible believers in alarming numbers are being painted into a corner by a wrong understanding of prophecy. Experience shows that if things do not turn out as their teachers are saying, people will doubt the credibility of the Bible and some may forsake the faith. On the other hand, some Christians try to avoid this trap by denying practically all literal Bible teaching. Posing as champions of truth, they offer a cure worse than the disease, misrepresenting the historic faith even more damagingly.

This book is sent forth to "contend earnestly for the faith which was once for all delivered to the saints" (Jude 3).[1]

It will not be necessary to define terms for readers familiar with prophecy jargon. Most Christians know that the word "millennium" means. 1,000 years and stands for the 1,000-year reign of Christ. The concept first appears in Revelation 20 and has since been interpreted in various ways. For many the millennium has come to mean a golden era during which Christ reigns over the earth—a time of peace, prosperity, long life, happiness, universal knowledge of God, harmony in the animal kingdom, earth producing enormous sizes and amounts of produce, and the like.

Three schools of interpretation need to be identified: postmillennial, premillennial, and amillennial. The postmillennial view is that Christ will return *after* the millennium. The premillennial, that He returns *before* it. The amillennial, that there is no millennium as such. Amillennialism is quite accurately described by one of its opponents quoting a kindred opponent:

> Its most general character is that of a denial of a literal reign of Christ upon the earth. Satan is conceived as bound at the first coming of Christ. The present age between the first and second comings is the fulfillment of the millennium. Its adherents differ as to whether the millennium is being fulfilled on the earth (Augustine) or whether it is being fulfilled by the saints in heaven (Warfield). It may be summed up in the idea that there will be no more millennium than there is now, and that the eternal state immediately follows the second coming of Christ. It is similar to postmillennialism in that Christ comes after what they regard as the millennium.[2]

To the premillennial classification above may be added the dispensational view which divides "the divine plan into dispensations during each of which God deals with the human race on the basis of some specific principle." So, here are four little labels, all in a row: "posties," "premies," "dispies," and "amies."

Several clarifications should be made.

1. A combination term that has been used is "dispensational premillennialism." It must be said, however, that "all Dispensationalists are Premillennialists, but not all Premillennialists are Dispensationalists."[3]

2. Modern premillennialism should be distinguished from what may be called historic premillennialism. It is commonly thought today in premillennial circles that the early church was premillennial. (The reader is referred to chapter 4 for treatment of that question.) Even if such a view was held by some, it needs to be stressed that these early premillennialists, for the most part, had a more spiritualized view of the millennium as a reign of Christ but not necessarily on earth. There were some exceptions, but they were considered extreme. The historic premillennial viewpoint continued to the present generation, as seen in the following example from a noted Lutheran scholar and seminary president:

> We do not venture to decide definitely where this reign will be established, whether in heaven or on earth. It is not stated

specifically, but the introduction of verse four [Revelation 20:4] seems to indicate that it is heaven.[4]

Historic premillennialism was described in much milder terms than today's view which goes by that name. It was more innocent. It was not so speculative; there was no secret rapture; no seven-year tribulation; and no restoration of national Israel. The church, composed of all races, was considered the true Israel. William Cox correctly observes that "there is very little resemblance between historic premillennialism and the premillennialism of our time."[5]

3. "Amillennialism" is an unfortunate term. It would be preferable to designate the three millennial schools as millennial, postmillennial and premillennial. The issue is not whether there is a millennium. The question is rather, *what* is it and *when* is it? Cox states the situation clearly:

> Amillennialism literally means "no millennium." This is an unfortunate term, however, since the great majority of amillennialists definitely do believe in a millennium based on Revelation 20:1-10. They simply rebel against the hyperliteralism placed on this passage by most of the other schools of millennialism. Amillennialists interpret Revelation 20:1-10 as representing the period of time between the two advents of our Lord, that is, as going on at the present time and ending when our Lord returns.[6]

After sketching the foregoing differences, it is important to add:

> In each of the three schools of thought concerning millennialism, there have been equally noble and conservative men. We might be surprised to find elements of truth in each of the camps. . . . Perhaps the wag was not too far afield when he coined a fourth title, "pan-millennialism," which simply holds that everything will pan out the way God wants it in the end.[7]

With a subject as vast as the millennium it is necessary to set some boundaries. The objective of this book is to give a rather comprehensive treatment of last things and the problem areas of interpretation. Of course one cannot, need not, and should not be exhaustive. One *cannot* be exhaustive, because time and the sheer volume of material involved do not allow it. It would take more worlds than this, to borrow from the imagery of John 21:25, to contain all that might be written. This writer's library section on this subject is quite voluminous. Many sources were not quoted in the interest of selectivity, brevity, and preciseness. One *need not* be exhaustive. After all, six examples demonstrate as effectively as would 66. As with effective painting, what is omitted requires as much good judgment as what is included. Every major passage and theme on things to come is treated. Representative arguments are employed instead of dealing with each Scripture bearing on the same point. The reader should make his own applications to related passages. One *should not* be exhaustive, because it would be exhausting both for the writer and for the reader. This is a weakness of much prophetic literature. There is a reason why Hal Lindsey's *The Late Great Planet Earth* has been translated into a score of languages—it really does not contain much theology but is current, interesting, and to the point, whether correct or not.

The teaching of Jesus on things to come is presented in chapter 1. The material of chapters 2—4 is arranged according to historical sequence, that is, Old Testament, apostles, church. Chapters 5—14 discuss various related topics.

The index of Scripture references should prove helpful to the reader, but bear in mind that, as in all sound theology, the parts should be interpreted in light of the whole.

CHAPTER 1

Things to Come
According to the Coming One

It seems almost impertinent to speak of the teaching of Jesus as if one were comparing His opinion with that of others. For the Christian the words of Jesus are not just opinion. They are the final word. What He says, being God, is altogether decisive. "For the testimony of Jesus is the spirit of prophecy" (Revelation 19:10). He says, "The Scriptures . . . bear witness of Me" (John 5:39). All Biblical revelation, all history, everything converges in Him and is given direction from Him, even as the cornerstone. He is *the* Word.

Just as the first commandment in essence embodies and comprises all the others, so what Jesus says is the basis of everything. Did not the Father at the Transfiguration testify from heaven saying, "This is My beloved Son, with whom I am well pleased; listen to Him" (Matthew 17:5 RSV). The fact that the Son of God was to be the source of all key revelation is seen also from the words of the woman who came to the well in Samaria to draw water. During her conversation with Jesus she said, "I know that Messiah is coming (He who is called Christ); when He comes He will show us all things" (John 4:25 RSV). He is indeed the light so that no one need be in darkness or misled. Jesus says that the wise build on "these words of Mine" (Matthew 7:24).

Jesus Christ . . . is the very substance, marrow, soul and scope of the whole Scriptures. What are the whole Scriptures, but as it were the spiritual swadling clothes of the Holy child Jesus. (1) Christ is the truth and substance of all types and shadows. (2) Christ is the matter and substance of the Covenant of Grace under all administrations thereof; under the Old Testament Christ is *veyled,* under the New Covenant *revealed.* (3) Christ is the

10

centre and meeting place of all the promises, for him Him all the promises of God are Yea, and they are Amen. (4) Christ is the thing signified, sealed, and exhibited in all the sacraments of the Old and New Testaments, whether ordinary or extraordinary. (5) Scripture genealogies are to lead us on to the true line of Christ. (6) Scripture chronologies are to discover to us the times and seasons of Christ. (7) Scripture laws are our schoolmaster to bring us to Christ; the moral by correcting, the ceremonial by directing. and (8) Scripture gospel is Christ's light, whereby we know Him; Christ's voice whereby we hear and follow Him; Christ's cords of love, whereby we are drawn into sweet union and communion with Him; yea, it is the power of God unto salvation unto all them that believe in Christ Jesus. Keep therefore still Jesus Christ in your eye, in the perusal of the Scripture, as the end, scope, and substance thereof. For as the sun gives light to all the heavenly bodies, so Jesus Christ the Sun of righteousness gives light to all the Holy Scriptures.[1]

Does Jesus teach an earthly millennium? If so, there must be one, and who would dare take it away? If not, how presumptious to add it.

A Survey of the Gospels and Acts 1

Matthew—Mark. After His baptism Jesus began His ministry, proclaiming, "Repent; for the kingdom of heaven is at hand" (Matthew 4:17). It is of vital importance to understand (1) what He meant by the kingdom of heaven, and (2) that it was at hand.

1. Dispensationalism distinguishes between the kingdom of God and the kingdom of heaven, a distinction lost in many passages that use the terms interchangeably. "Dispensationalists build much of their argument upon the assumption that the kingdom of God and the kingdom of heaven are two separate kingdoms."[2] This position is shown by the following example:

> In the Gospel according to Matthew this kingdom is designated in the main as the kingdom of heaven, whereas the kingdom of God is mentioned but a few times. . . . Mark and Luke, on the other hand, are writing to Gentiles, so they use the phrase "kingdom of God" rather than the other.[3]

Several Scriptures will suffice to show the inconsistency of this

11

idea. "Jesus came . . . saying, '. . . the kingdom of God is at hand . . . .'" The parallel passage is Matthew 4:17: "The kingdom of heaven is at hand." Note that the terms "kingdom of God" and "kingdom of heaven" are used interchangeably and with the same audience—and this by inspiration of the Holy Spirit. Even more telling is an example of our Lord's usage of both terms in the same breath, as it were:

> Jesus said to His disciples, "Truly I say to you, it is hard for a rich man to enter the kingdom of heaven. And again I say to you, it is easier for a camel to go through the eye of a needle, than for a rich man to enter the kingdom of God (Matthew 19:23-24).

Surely no one would try to divide between this utterance as if in the first half He spoke of a rich Jew, and in the second a rich Gentile. The difference in terminology may be traced to modes of expression more common to one writer than to another.

However, it is important *not* to make the terms mean that there were two kingdoms:

> Before one can correctly understand the teachings of Scripture concerning God's kingdom, the fact must be established that God has but *one* kingdom. While this kingdom is referred to by different terms in the Bible (kingdom of God, kingdom of heaven, kingdom of our Lord, kingdom of Christ), all such terms are used interchangeably, and each term is synonymous, describing one and the same eternal kingdom.[4]

2. The "at hand" aspect of the kingdom was Jesus' fundamental message for Judaism and for the world. It was and is "at hand" in Him.[5] Instead of setting forth in detail the nonmaterialistic nature of that kingdom, let this suffice: "The kingdom of God is not eating and drinking, but righteousness and peace and joy in the Holy Spirit" (Romans 14:17).[6] The kingdom is not materialistic, but no less real. It is substantial and enduring, to be enjoyed at last in resurrected bodies.

Contrary to the clear words of Jesus and the Scriptures, dispensationalism teaches that Christ came to establish a theocratic, earthly kingdom, that He offered Himself as king to the Jewish people, but that that offer was refused, and so the kingdom was postponed. Such an idea raises serious problems. For one thing, the Jewish people were under Rome at the time. When faced with the "king of the Jews" accusation, the Lord answered Pilate, "My kingdom is not of this world. . . . My kingdom is not of this realm" (John 18:36). Another difficulty in interpreting the kingdom dispensationally is encountered with Christ's own declarations as to His mission, e.g., "The Son of Man did not come to be served, but to serve and to give His life as a ransom for many" (Mark 10:45). "Such statements," it is observed, "cannot be reconciled with the Dispensational scheme."[7] Such a scheme meets further difficulty in the fact that Jesus refused that kingship. "Jesus therefore perceiving that they were intending to come and take Him by force to make Him king, withdrew again to the mountain by Himself alone" (John 6:15). As for His triumphal entry into Jerusalem (Matthew 21; Mark 11; Luke 19; John 12), it was not as in the Scofield Bible heading of Matthew 21: "The King's public offer of himself as King,"[8] but an accepting of worship as the true heavenly king. These and other insuperable difficulties abound—notably a pre-Calvary unredeemed kingdom—if the kingdom progression is thought to have taken this route.

> To the Christian who realizes the meaning of the Cross, who knows that he has been redeemed by the precious blood of Christ, the question raised by the Dispensational interpretation of the words "at hand" is of the greatest moment. It amounts to this, Could men have been saved without the Cross?[9]

And as for the kingdom *postponement,* note what happens to those who refuse Christ as Savior, be they Jew or Gentile, e.g., as described in Luke 19:11-27 in Christ's parable of the nobleman who left to receive a kingdom, returned, and ordered all rebels slain!

Christ's teaching regarding the course of world history allows for no dispensational break of progression from His earthly ministry to His final advent.

> In the parables of the wheat and tares and of the net (Matthew 13:24-30, 36-43, and 47-50), the Lord is giving, as all admit, a picture of this gospel age, which closes with His second coming.

In the kingdom, the wheat and tares are to grow together till the harvest at the end of the world.[10]

Following is the parable of the wheat and tares, Matthew 13:24-30. Jesus' explanation of it is given in verses 36-43 of the same chapter.

He presented another parable to them, saying, "The kingdom of heaven may be compared to a man who sowed good seed in his field. But while men were sleeping, his enemy came and sowed tares also among the wheat, and went away. But when the wheat sprang up and bore grain, then the tares became evident also. And the slaves of the landowner came and said to him, 'Sir, did you not sow good seed in your field? How then does it have tares?' And he said to them, 'An enemy has done this!' And the slaves said to him, 'Do you want us, then, to go and gather them up?' But he said, 'No; lest while you are gathering up the tares, you may root up the wheat with them. Allow both to grow together until the harvest; and in the time of harvest I will say to the reapers, "First gather up the tares and bind them in bundles to burn them up; but father the wheat into my barn."'"

Note also the parable of the net from the same chapter:

Again, the kingdom of heaven is like a drag-net cast into the sea, and gathering fish of every kind; and when it was filled, they drew it up on the beach; and they sat down, and gathered the good fish into containers, but the bad they threw away. So it will be at the end of the age; the angels shall come forth, and take out the wicked from among the righteous, and will cast them into the furnace of fire; there shall be weeping and gnashing of teeth (Matthew 13:47-50).

Once again, observe the unbroken progression without introduction of dispensations.

The Savior constantly speaks from the vantage point of His first advent and spans all-inclusive history to the end of the world, without mention of interruptions or periods intervening. In our survey of Matthew-Mark we come now to Matthew 16:24-28 and 19:27-29, passages similar in content:

Then Jesus said to His disciples, "If anyone wishes to come after Me, let him deny himself, and take up his cross, and follow

Me. For whoever wishes to save his life shall lose it; but whoever loses his life for My sake shall find it. For what will a man be profited, if he gains the whole world, and forfeits his soul? Or what will a man give in exchange for his soul? For the Son of Man is going to come in the glory of His father with His angels; and will then recompense every man according to his deeds. Truly I say to you, there are some of those who are standing here who shall not taste death until they see the Son of Man coming in His kingdom."

Then Peter answered and said to Him, "Behold, we have left everything and followed You; what then will there be for us?" And Jesus said to them, "Truly I say to you, that you who have followed Me, in the regeneration when the Son of Man will sit on His glorious throne, you also shall sit upon twelve thrones, juding the twelve tribes of Israel."

Note that the closing verse in the former example would have been proved incorrect if the "kingdom" were an earthly Palestine. It must refer rather to a nonpersonal manifestation, a coming into His kingdom of power such as in Pentecost, in the destruction of Jerusalem, and the like. But the point to observe is the unbroken movement toward the final recompense. The second reference above may seem to lend credence to the idea of some special kingdom—"twelve thrones, judging the twelve tribes"[11]—however, it need not mean that, for it does not suggest an intervening period, but a final judgment, and is just as true if so applied. There are other wondrous matters to ponder concerning the judgment, a many-sided theme. For instance, 1 Corinthians 6:2-3: "Or do you not know that the saints will judge the world? . . . Do you not know that we shall judge angels?"

Another insight into the eschatology of our Lord regarding His own Jewish people is given in the parable of the wicked tenant farmers:

"Listen to another parable. There was a landowner who planted a vineyard and put a wall around it and dug a wine press in it,and built a tower, and rented it out to vine-growers, and went on a journey. And when the harvest time approached, he sent his slaves to the vine-growers to receive his produce. And the vine-growers took his slaves and beat one, and killed another, and stoned a third. Again he sent another group of slaves larger than the first; and they did the same thing to them. But afterward he sent his son to them saying, 'They will respect my son.' But when the vine-growers saw the son, they said among themselves, 'This is the heir; come, let us kill him, and seize his inheritance.' And they took him, and cast him out of the vineyard, and killed him. Therefore when the owner of the vineyard comes, what will he do to those vine-growers?" They said to Him, "He will bring those wretches to a wretched end, and will rent out the vineyard to other vine-growers, who will pay him the proceeds at the proper seasons." Jesus said to them, "Did you never read in the Scriptures, 'The stone which the builders rejected, this became the chief corner stone; this came about from the Lord, and it is marvelous in our eyes'? Therefore I say to you, the kingdom of God will be taken away from you, and be given to a nation producing the fruit of it. And he who falls on this stone will be broken to pieces; but on whomever it falls, it will scatter him like dust" (Matthew 21:33-44).

When he comes, the wicked will not be given the kingdom but will suffer a wretched end. Further, the words "journey" and "harvest time" show that the meaning cannot be confined to the A.D. 70 destruction but suggest even more strongly the final end.

The next chapter, with the parable of the marriage feast (Matthew 22:1-14), likewise foretells destruction, without mention of a coming kingdom age.

Matthew 23:39 presents a thought often used to support the notion of a coming millennial kingdom. Jesus says: "I say to you, from now on you shall not see Me until you say, 'Blessed is He who comes in the name of the Lord.'" Thankfully it can be noted that this prophecy does not await a future fulfillment but is accomplished each time a formerly unreceptive person receives Jesus as Savior.

But their minds were hardened; for until this very day at the reading of the old covenant the same veil remains unlifted, because it is removed in Christ. But to this day whenever Moses is read, a veil lies over their heart; but whenever a man turns to the Lord, the veil is taken away (2 Corinthians 3:14-16).

The veil fell away from many Jews in that day as it has for many

Jews in this day. Even Jewish historians have estimated there were nearly two million Jewish converts to Christianity during the first century after Christ. When they look on the pierced One, they are gathered "The way a hen gathers her chicks under her wings" (Matthew 23:37). This is exactly the thought brought out by Peter with John at the Beautiful Gate of the temple:

> "Men of Israel, why do you marvel at this, or why do you gaze at us, as if by our own power or piety we had made him walk?... God . . . has glorified . . . Jesus, the one whom you delivered up, and disowned in the presence of Pilate . . . . But the things which God announced beforehand by the mouth of all the prophets, that His Christ should suffer, He has thus fulfilled. Repent therefore and return, that your sins may be wiped away, in order that times of refreshing may come from the presence of the Lord; and that He may send Jesus, the Christ appointed for you, whom heaven must receive until the period of restoration of all things about which God spoke by the mouth of His holy prophets from ancient time. Moses said, "The Lord God shall raise up for you a prophet like me from your brethren; to Him you shall give heed in everything He says to you. And it shall be that every soul that does not heed that prophet shall be utterly destroyed from among the people.' And likewise, all the prophets who have spoken, from Samuel and his successors onward, also announced these days. It is you who are the sons of the prophets, and of the covenant which God made with your fathers, saying to Abraham, 'And in your seed all the families of the earth shall be blessed.' For you first, God raised up His Servant, and sent Him to bless you by turning every one of you from your wicked ways" (Acts 3:12-26).

At Matthew 24 one stands before a great body of prophetic truth uttered by our Lord. In approaching it, one should bear in mind that a prophecy can have a near and a far fulfillment, as Ramm says: "The destruction of Jerusalem is prophesied by our Lord and through it we have a perspective through which to envision the end of the world."[12] In Matthew 24:3 the disciples inquire as to His coming and the end of the age. Again it should be noted that they make no mention of the start of another earthly age after this present age.

Verses 9-14 sketch the general course of the world. Note that there is no break anywhere from that day to the end:

> "Then they will deliver you up to tribulation, and will kill you, and you will be hated by all nations on account of My name. And at that time many will fall away and will betray one another and hate one another. And many false prophets will arise, and will mislead many. And because lawlessness is increased, most people's love will grow cold. But the one who endures to the end, it is he who shall be saved. And this gospel of the kingdom shall be preached in the whole world for a witness to all the nations, and then the end shall come."

Verse 15: "When you see the abomination of desolation which was spoken of through Daniel the prophet, standing in the holy place . . . ." This verse may be understood as referring to the destruction of Jerusalem in 70 A.D.

> The "abomination of desolation" is a Hebrew expression, signifying "abominable, or hateful destroyer." Where Daniel uses the word abomination, Christ adds the word "desolation," because it was to make Jerusalem utterly desolate. As Luke in this connection speaks of the compassing of Jerusalem with armies, I think it clear that, by the abomination of desolation, the Savior meant to designate the Roman armies. These were composed of soldiers who were idolaters. They carried in front of their legions ensigns or standards upon which were painted the images of eagles and of their emperors. These, Suetonius informs us, the Romans worshipped; whilst Tacitus calls them "the gods of war." Chrysostom says, "that every idol and every image of a man was by the Jews called an abomination." An illustration is mentioned by Josephus: that "when Vitellius, the governor of Syria, was conducting his army through Judea, against Aretas, the king of the Arabians, the principal Jews, on account of their strong abhorrence of the ensigns of the soldiers, on which were eagles and the images of the emperors, earnestly entreated him to lead his army some other way, and that he greatly obliged them by complying with their request." In corroboration of the fact that the Romans worshipped these standards, Josephus adds, "that after the city was taken, the Romans brought their ensigns into the temple, and placed them opposite the eastern gate, and sacrificed to them in that place." The Roman armies are properly called the abomination of desolation, as desolation marked their

advances through all the provinces and nations they had subdued, and as by them the holy city, and its more holy temple, were to be utterly destroyed.[13]

A most enlightening explanation along the same lines is given in a lengthy excerpt from Eusebius, bishop of Caesarea, born about A.D. 260:

The whole body, however, of the church of Jerusalem, having been commanded by a divine revelation, given to men of approved piety there before the war, removed from the city, and dwelt at a certain town beyond the Jordan, called Pella. Here, those that believed in Christ, having removed from Jerusalem, as if holy men had entirely abandoned the royal city itself, and the whole land of Judea: the divine justice, for their crimes against Christ and his apostles, finally overtook them, totally destroying the whole generation of these evil-doers from the earth. But the number of calamities which then overwhelmed the whole nation; the extreme misery to which particularly the inhabitants of Judea were reduced; the vast numbers of men, with women and children that fell by the sword and famine, and innumerable other forms of death; the numerous and great cities of Judea that were besieged, as also the great and incredible distresses that they experienced who took refuge at Jerusalem, as a place of perfect security; these facts, as well as the whole tenor of the war, and each particular of its progress, when, finally, the abomination of desolation, according to the prophetic declaration, stood in the very temple of God, so celebrated of old, but which now was approaching its total downfall and final destruction by fire; all this, I say, any one that wishes may see accurately stated in the history written by Josephus. It may, however, be necessary to state, in the very words of this writer, how about three hundred thousand that flocked from all parts of Judea at the time of the passover, were shut up in Jerusalem as in a prison. For it was indeed just, that in those very days in which they had inflicted sufferings upon the Saviour and Benefactor of all men, the Christ of God, destruction should overtake them, thus shut up as in a prison, as an exhibition of the divine justice. Passing by then, the particular calamities which befell them, such as they suffered from the sword, and other means employed against them I may deem it sufficient only to subjoin the calamities they endured from the famine. So that they who peruse the present history may know, in some measure, that the divine vengeance did not long delay to visit them for their iniquity against the Christ of God.[14]

Verse 21 speaks of "a great tribulation." This is a reference to the pre-A. D. 70 generation and a prophecy of the end time—the former evident in verse 20: " . . . your flight . . . in the winter, or on a Sabbath," the latter evident in verses 22 ff., the meaning of which cannot be confined to that first Christian century but extends to the end of the world.

Verse 27 must be compared with Luke 17:20-37, which intertwines A. D. 70 and the end almost indistinguishably. The "eagles" suggest the Roman army insignia.

Verse 29 does not speak of an extended time but of the end coming "immediately after the tribulation of those days," as the universe disintegrates. In that awesome moment also—verses 30-31—the Son of Man comes, sending His angels with a loud trumpet call. One who formerly held and taught the dispensational view but now disclaims it in complete support of the nonearthly millennium position writes:

> The Bible, the Church Fathers, the Great Historic Church Creeds, the Great Reformers, the true teachers everywhere teach but one future bodily coming, the Second Advent, which is visible and noisy. 1 Thess. 4:14-17; 2 Peter 3:10-17. This is the Rapture of the Church, and for His Church; angels and the souls of departed saints will accompany Him as He descends from Heaven; at the sound of the trumpet, as Christ descends, the souls of the righteous dead are reunited with their bodies (this is the resurrection day), the saints living upon earth shall suddenly be changed and, together with the resurrected, shall arise to meet Him in the air to accompany Him to earth when He executes judgment upon the wicked. They shall forever be with Him. Hebrews 9:28; John 5:28, 29; 1 Cor. 6:2; 15:51-56; 1 Thess. 3:13; 4:14-17; Jude 14; Rev. 1:17.[15]

Again it should be noted that in all the prophetic teaching of this chapter Christ never speaks of an intervening earthly kingdom age. Furthermore, He tells of the days of Noah, with one taken and another left (in the destruction). The parallel in Luke 17 intertwines A. D. 70 and the end. This points up the fact that there is nothing such as a rapture and earthly millennium coming between that time (when these words were spoken) and the end.

There may be an insight from verse 34 ("this generation") coupled with the intertwining of A. D. 70 and the end. If the Jewish people (though a mixed race now) are meant by "this generation," it could be that the Jewish return to Palestine (in 1948) and Jerusalem surrounded is a sign for us to lift up our heads in anticipation of our redemption soon. But if so, that does not mean that a millennium will follow.

The three parables of Matthew 25 (Ten Virgins, Talents, Judgment) stress preparedness and reward or loss, issuing in final destinies of either eternal punishment or eternal life. Unless something is imported from the outside and made to complicate the simplicity of these teachings, one would understand only an unbroken progression to a single final advent; nor would one find in these parables, supposedly, a complicated, confusing distinction between Jews and Gentiles.

In Matthew 26 Jesus speaks of not drinking again of the fruit of the vine "until that day when I drink it new with you in My Father's kingdom" (verse 29). Mark's parallel (14:25) quotes the Lord as saying "kingdom of God." The reader is referred back to previous references in this chapter to see the folly of distinguishing the terms dispensationally as if the "kingdom" or "kingdom of heaven" and the "kingdom of God" were different entities.

Finally, the Great Commission of Matthew 28 extends to the close of the age, without mention of any other age coming before eternity. It contains also our Lord's tremendous declaration, "All authority has been given to Me in heaven and on earth" (verse 18). Lawrence Thomas well remarks:

> After His resurrection Jesus said, "All power (authority, R.S.V.) is given unto Me in heaven and in earth" (Matthew 28:18). How much power and authority? "All!" Where? "In heaven and in earth!"[16]

Luke. As a synoptic gospel, Luke requires little additional treatment in this survey. References to various parallel passages have been made already.

It may be noted in the annunciation to Mary that "the throne of David" is mentioned, and "the house of Jacob" and that "of His kingdom there will be no end." This cannot refer to a kingdom age of limited duration. "His Kingdom is never said to be a 1,000-year Kingdom, but always an everlasting Kingdom."[17]

Reference has been made previously to Luke 17 and how clearly the Savior sets forth therein that the day of grace continues from His first advent to the day of destruction, uninterrupted by a 1,000-year rule over the earth administered by Him from a Palestinian headquarters at Jerusalem.

Also, in this chapter we have treated Luke 21 in connection with its Matthew 24 and Mark 13 parallels. Luke 21:24 needs further comment:

> They will fall by the edge of the sword, and will be led captive into all the nations; and Jerusalem will be trampled underfoot by the Gentiles until the times of the Gentiles be fulfilled.

Once again it must be said that neither this passage nor Romans 11:25 teaches that Jerusalem is to have a further history after the so-called times of the Gentiles. Unless that idea is brought in from elsewhere there is no reason to think that the "until" indicates something earthly following for Jerusalem, a fiction about which Jesus says nothing. (See chapter 10 for further explanation.)

John. Jesus' eschatology as reported by John gives us additional insight as to the resurrection (5:24-28; 6:39-40, 54; 11:1-44), as well as to the final judgment and eternal life.

In John 3 Jesus speaks of the nature of the kingdom. It is real but spiritual.

In John 14 He says:

> Let not your heart be troubled: ye believe in God, believe also in Me. In My Father's house are many mansions: if it were not so, I would have told you. I go to prepare a place for you. And if I go and prepare a place for you, I will come again, and receive you unto Myself; that where I am, there ye may be also (verses 1-3 KJV).

This simple, beautiful assurance need not be treated further eschatologically..

John 16 contains an explanation of the mission and work of the Holy Spirit to come, starting at Pentecost.

John 17 gives added insight into Christ's preexistence, preincarnate state, and the future glory.

John 18:36 again gives the nondispensational insight:

> Jesus answered, "My kingdom is not of this world. If My kingdom were of this world, then My servants would be fighting, that I might not be delivered up to the Jews; but as it is, My kingdom is not of this realm."

Acts 1. Except for His special appearance to Saul on the Damascus road and His speaking in the Book of Revelation, the first chapter of Acts contains the final words of Jesus.

In Acts 1:6 (RSV) the disciples ask, "Lord, will you at this time restore the kingdom to Israel?" On the surface this sounds as if an earthly millennium may have been expected by the apostles. Christ dismisses this, saying, "It is not for you to know times or epochs." They were to win converts from among Jews and Gentiles. Here is a helpful comment on the matter:

> The kingdom to be proclaimed under the terms of the Great Commission was "the kingdom of God." It was not to be Israelitish: it was to be world-embracing. This was the answer to the question as it related to Israel.[18]

Conclusion

The testimony of Jesus should be accepted as the truth, the whole truth, and nothing but the truth, full and final, for He is God. Both Testaments must agree in Him. None must take away from nor add to the perfect deposit of our Lord's teachings. Lawrence Thomas gives a wise caution in that regard:

> We are not to instruct people about future events which the Lord Jesus has not endorsed. Neither are we to set ourselves up as teachers of prophetical things which contradict His predictions

23

(Matthew 12:36-42). A golden rule is: Where Christ is silent we ought to be silent also.

. . . .

It is the height of folly to run ahead of Him who is our Master. None of the Apostles added an opposing doctrine but did expand His.

. . . .

Be convinced, once and for all, that our Lord's method of interpretation should be the Christian's method. We must give Him the credit for knowing the Old Testament better than we do. Everything He said about the Kingdom, the people who inherit it, and who were then entering it, comes direct from the Old Testament prophets. Christ is the Divine Interpreter.[19]

Such thoughts serve to reinforce the theme of this book. Only the First and the Last knows the last things.

One certainly shares Christian sentiments of good will toward godly people who love the Bible. No matter what system of prophetic interpretation they have been taught they are loved by our Lord Jesus Christ.

It gives us no pleasure, but rather sorrow, to make these observations; but we feel that a devotion to Christ and His truth must take precedence over our deference to our fellow man, however highly regarded by ourselves and others.

There was but one kingdom offered by our Lord Jesus Christ. He offers that kingdom to all who will enter into it today. . . . When He comes again He will call His people to Himself to "inherit the Kingdom prepared for you from the foundation of the world (Matthew 25:34)." That kingdom will not be Palestine, anymore than it will be Poland. . . . We cannot think of any proof that should be more conclusive in this respect than the silence of the New Testament regarding any such kingdom. The whole thought is foreign to the revelation given by Jesus Christ.[20]

There is something pathetic about those who spiritualize away all reality and those who are blinded to the transcendent by hyperliteralism. Christ is coming, literally! He is the coming King. But "there are no literal thrones for Deity."[21]

There will not be an earthly political millennium during the course of history. Multitudes of Jews and Gentiles will not be

24

saved after His coming. The eschatology of Jesus our Lord most emphatically rules out any possibility of salvation for even one soul after His coming.

As He comes, His church is caught away—raptured—as the world ends and the universe is refashioned. The final judgment ensues. Eternal destinies follow. "When He comes eternity comes." [22]

Nowhere in the teachings of our Lord does one find an earthly reign of 1,000 years before or after His final advent.

CHAPTER 2

Things to Come and the Old Testament

> "While the earth remains,
> Seedtime and harvest,
> And cold and heat,
> And summer and winter,
> And day and night
> Shall not cease" (Genesis 8:22).

That was the first indication in the Old Testament that the days of the earth were numbered. But the means of its destruction would not again be water.

> I establish My covenant with you; and all flesh shall never again
> be cut off by the waters of the flood, neither shall there again be
> a flood to destroy the earth (Genesis 9:11).

There would not be multiple destructions—only one. "Thus says the Lord of hosts, Once more in a little while, I am going to shake the heavens and the earth, the sea also and the dry land" (Haggai 2:6).

> His voice shook the earth then, but now He has promised, saying, "Yet once more I will shake not only the earth, but also the heaven." And this expression, "Yet once more," denotes the removing of those things which can be shaken, as of created things, in order that those things which cannot be shaken may remain. Therefore, since we receive a kingdom which cannot be shaken, let us show gratitude, by which we may offer to God an acceptable service with reverence and awe; for our God is a consuming fire (Hebrews 12:26-39).

Our procedure in this chapter will be first to treat prophecies pertaining to the physical end of the world and the refashioning of the universe for eternity. Then the study will turn to the agenda of history to that point, with attendant problems of interpretation.

The End and Thereafter

It was a dim conception, but under the Old Covenant there was hope beyond the grave. The repeated phrase, "he slept with his fathers," indicated survival beyond death. Moses, Solomon, Daniel, and others spoke of judgment and of books of life (examples: Exodus 32:32-33; Ecclesiastes 11:19; 12:14; Daniel 7:10).

Hope of the resurrection, a term that inherently means resurrection of the body, was held under the Old Testament too, as seen from such passages as Daniel 12:2-3; Job 19:25-27; Psalms 71:20-21; 73:24-26; Jeremiah 31:15-17; Isaiah 66:24; Hosea 13:14.

The "how" of the earth's end is to be by fire, as seen throughout holy Scripture. Old Testament references to that include:

> Neither their silver nor their gold
> Will be able to deliver them
> On the day of the Lord's wrath;
> And all the earth will be devoured
> In the fire of His jealousy,
> For He will make a complete end,

Indeed a terrifying one,
Of all the inhabitants of the earth (Zephaniah 1:18).

For behold, the Lord will come in fire
And his chariots like the whirlwind,
To render His anger with fury,
And His rebuke with flames of fire.
For the Lord will execute judgment by fire
And by His sword on all flesh,
And those slain by the Lord will be many (Isaiah 66:15-16).

Behold, the day of the Lord is coming,
Cruel, with fury and burning anger,
To make the land a desolation;
And He will exterminate its sinners from it.
For the stars of heaven and their constellations
Will not flash forth their light;
The sun will be dark when it rises,
And the moon will not shed its light.
Thus I will punish the world for its evil,
And the wicked for their iniquity;
I will also put an end to the arrogance of the proud,
And abase the haughtiness of the ruthless.
I will make mortal man scarcer than pure gold,
And mankind than the gold of Ophir.
Therefore I shall make the heavens tremble,
And the earth will be shaken from its place
At the fury of the Lord of hosts
In the day of His burning anger (Isaiah 13:9-13).

And all the host of heaven will wear away,
And the sky will be rolled up like a scroll;
All their hosts will also wither away
As a leaf withers from the vine,
Or as one withers from the fig tree (Isaiah 34:4).

"Lift up your eyes to the sky,
Then look to the earth beneath;
For the sky will vanish like smoke,
And the earth will wear out like a garment,
And its inhabitants will die in like manner,
But my salvation shall be forever,
And my righteousness shall not wane (Isaiah 51:6).

This destruction of the world would be followed by the endless ages of eternity as is seen by these sample passages from Isaiah:

"For behold, I create new heavens and a new earth;
And the former things shall not be remembered
    or come to mind" (Isaiah 65:17).

"For just as the new heavens and the new earth
Which I make will endure before Me,"
declares the Lord,
"So your offspring and your name will endure.
"And it shall be from new moon to new moon
And from sabbath to sabbath,
All mankind will come to bow down before Me,"
    says the Lord (Isaiah 66:22-23).

In the Meantime

Here is where the headwaters divide between the schools of interpretation. Dispensationalism divides the Bible or God's administration into seven dispensations and eight covenants. According to that system, the present *dispensation* is grace, with the kingdom dispensation still to come; and the present *covenant* is the New, with the Palestinian and Davidic to be reestablished.

However, the Bible, or God's dealing revolves around but two dispensations, Law and Gospel. Also there are but two basic covenants, the Old and New, and essentially they are but one—everything converging in Christ.

Abrahamic considerations. Dispensationalsim makes much of the so-called Abrahamic and Davidic covenants, stressing the former as a land promise (to Jews) and the latter as the promise of a millennial kingdom (with Christ reigning at Jerusalem).

To be sure, Abraham was promised a Seed and land, but in realization these were to be greater than he could conceive. That Abraham understood these promises in that greater-than-earthly sense is seen, for example, in Hebrews 11:10: "For he looked forward to the city which has foundations, whose builder and maker is God."

Davidic considerations. The Davidic concept of the kingdom will be traced in more detail. David intended to build a temple, a house for the Lord. But through Nathan the Lord tells David of His own "house" plan:

> The LORD also tells you He will build a house for you. When your time is up, and you lie down with your ancestors, I will give you a Descendant who will come from you, and I will establish His kingdom. He will build a temple for My name, and I will make the throne of His kingdom stand forever. I will be His Father, and He will be My Son. If He sins, I will punish Him with the rod of men and with blows inflicted by men. But I will not stop being kind to Him as I did to Saul whom I put out of your way. Your royal house will stand firm before Me forever, and your throne will stand firm forever (2 Samuel 7:11-16 WFB).

In order to maintain historical continuity, the covenant incorporated both temporal and eternal aspects of the kingdom. Accordingly the promise had to be clarified and modified. This adjustment is apparent in the Chronicles, written several hundred years later. That the eternal kingdom was not to be established by a procreated son of David himself is seen from 1 Chronicles 17:11:

> And it shall come about when your days are fulfilled that you must go to be with your father, that I will set up one of your descendants after you, who shall be of your sons; and I will establish his kingdom.

The Davidic kingdom promise was not forgotten; for example, "In the coronation ritual each king was hailed as the adopted 'son' of Yahweh . . . ."[1] This helped keep alive popular hope in the certainty and unchanging nature of the Davidic promise.

Since a mix of divine and human factors was involved, no wonder that such a passage as Psalm 89 has repeated parallel references to both *chesed* (mercy) and *berith* (covenant). Verses 30-36 especially will serve to confirm what has been said to now:

> If his children should forsake My law, and walk not in My judgments; if they should profane My ordinances, and not keep My commandments; I will visit their transgressions with a rod, and their sins with scourges. But My mercy I will not utterly remove from him, nor wrong My truth. Neither will I by any means profane My covenant; and I will not make void the things

that proceed out of My lips. Once have I sworn by My holiness, that I will not lie to David. His seed shall endure for ever (LXX).

The division of the kingdoms of Israel and Judah, ending the unity achieved under David; the captivities and returns; the helpless, rudderless intertestamental period: all were refining fires to teach the hope of a better and enduring kingdom. So was the Lord Jesus Christ awaited. Many mistakenly awaited Him in a materialistic kingdom sense. But those who awaited Him in the heavenly, eternal sense understood His kingdom aright, as do those who properly await Him now. His kingdom is not of this world.

The fundamental misunderstanding of dispensational premillennialism regarding the land and kingdom promise has to do with type and duration. The true Israel's inheritance is not to be *Palestine* but the *new earth*. The kingdom is not to be limited to 1,000 years, ending with destruction. *Over and over again the contexts of the supposed millennial kingdom passages use the word "forever";* therefore they cannot be applied to a 1,000-year period.

Contradictions abound in the system that looks for a physical millennium. And while it is true that the nonphysical millennium position is also not without problems, it is wise to choose the lesser difficulties.

Inconsistencies, large and small, are seen at every hand in the dispensational system. Isaiah 2, for example, is supposed to speak of an earthly millennial kingdom:

"Nation will not lift up sword against nation,
And never again will they learn war" (Isaiah 2:4).

But that can apply only to the eternal kingdom of Christ, for the earthly millennial kingdom must end in the most fearful war of history, Gog and Magog II, no less! The only way out of this conundrum would be for the earthly kingdom adherents to explain, "Well, nations will never again *learn* war, that is, take schooling in war; they will have to fight the big one without military training."

Isaiah 2 and 11 are said to speak of the millennial kingdom when

"The wolf will dwell with the lamb
And the leopard will lie down with the kid,
And the calf and the young lion and the fatling together;
And a little boy will lead them" (Isaiah 11:6).

The parallel passage to Isaiah 2 is Micah 4:1-7, which, however, speaks instead of the eternal kingdom, as the final verse shows:

But in the last days it shall come to pass, that the mountain of the house of the Lord shall be established in the top of the mountains, and it shall be exalted above the hills; and people shall flow unto it. . . . And he shall judge among many people, and rebuke strong nations afar off; and they shall beat their swords into plowshares, and their spears into pruninghooks: nation shall not lift up a sword against nation, neither shall they learn war any more. . . . And I will make her that halted a remnant, and her that was cast far off a strong nation: and the Lord shall reign over them in a mount Zion from henceforth, even for ever (KJV).

Daniel 9. Daniel is given an explanation of the history of his people until Christ and His eternal kingdom. How simple when taken naturally without break or gap.
Verse 24 reads:

Seventy weeks have been determined upon thy people, and upon the holy city, for sin to be ended, and to seal up transgressions, and to blot out the iniquities, and to make atonement for iniquities, and to bring in everlasting righteousness, and to seal the vision and the prophet, and to anoint the Most Holy (LXX).

Literally the opening of verse 24 would be rendered, "seventy sevens." The clue to correct understanding of the vision was within the grasp of a familiar exponent of dispensationalism:

The Hebrew word is *shabua,* which means literally a "seven" and it would be well to read the passage thus, dropping for a moment the word "week" which to the English ear always means a week of days. Thus the twenty-fourth verse of Daniel's ninth chapter simply asserts that "seventy sevens are determined."[2]

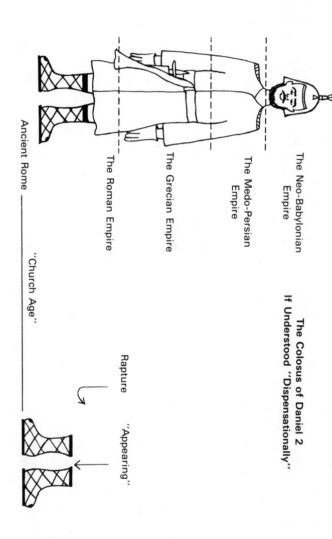

The Colosus of Daniel 2
If Understood "Dispensationally"

The Neo-Babylonian Empire

The Medo-Persian Empire

The Grecian Empire

The Roman Empire

Ancient Rome

"Church Age"

Rapture

"Appearing"

32

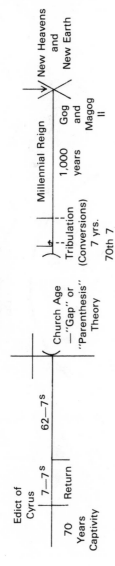

Daniel 9:24-27
"Dispensationally"

Edict of Cyrus

70 Years Captivity

$7-7^s$ | Return

$62-7^s$

Church Age —"Gap" or "Parenthesis" Theory

Tribulation (Conversions) 7 yrs.

70th 7

Millennial Reign

1,000 years

Gog and Magog II

New Heavens and New Earth

Daniel 9:24-27
"Seventy Sevens"
(Scripturally Correct)

Edict of Cyrus

70 Years Captivity

$7-7^s$ | Return

$62-7^s$

70th "7"

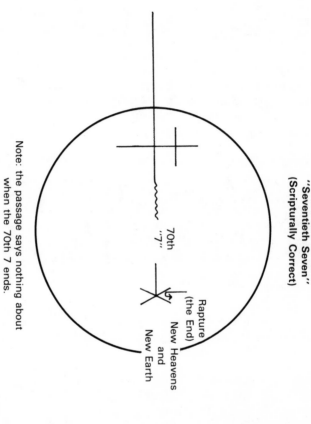

Daniel 9:24-27
"Seventieth Seven"
(Scripturally Correct)

70th
"7"

Rapture
(the End)
New Heavens
and
New Earth

ETERNITY

Note: the passage says nothing about
when the 70th 7 ends.

In the splendid commentary by Edward J. Young this fact of "seventy sevens" is correctly handled—not "seventy weeks (of years)," as in most translations, but "seventy sevens." The 70th seven should be thought of as an entire Christian era, of undetermined length, between Christ's first and final advents. The extent of the 70th seven necessarily is unknown if the time of the final advent was to be unknown. Thus Christ's coming has been ever "at hand" though seemingly long delayed.[3]

One senses the genius of the Holy Spirit in conceiving of these "seventy sevens." A misunderstanding of them allows for the "gap" or "parenthesis" theory, i.e., that the present church age is an unforeseen affair between the 69th and 70th weeks of Daniel. The 70th week is said to be yet future! In the dispensational scheme of things, it cannot begin until after Christ comes and takes the chruch away from the earth (rapture). It is then that a revived Roman Empire (European Common Market) is to emerge, according to the dispensational interpretation of Daniel 2. That chapter pictured a great image, a colossus. But if said view were correct, the feet and toes are not confined under the image but rather (since they were to be future) are removed from the body by the distance of the "gap" which will soon have extended to 2,000 years!

Here is a helpful summary of how the passage is to be understood simply:

> In response to his prayer, Gabriel announces to Daniel that a period of sevens—the exact length of the seven is not stated—in fact, seventy of them, has been decreed for the purpose of accomplishing the Messianic work. This Messianic work is described both in negative and positive terms; negative— restraining the transgression, completing sin and covering iniquity; positive—bringing in everlasting righteousness, sealing vision and prophet and anointing a holy of holies.
>
> Daniel therefore is to know and understand that from the going forth of a word to restore and build Jerusalem unto an anointed one who is also a prince (i.e., a royal priest) is seven sevens and sixty and two sevens. We are not told when this word went forth from the Lord but the effects of its issuance first appear in the return from bondage during the first year of Cyrus. This period is divided into two. The first period of seven sevens is evidently intended to include the time from the first year of

Cyrus to the completion of the work of Ezra and Nehemiah, and the second that from the completion of the work of Ezra and Nehemiah unto the first advent of Christ who alone can be described as an anointed one, a prince. During this entire period the city will be completely rebuilt, although this will be accomplished during times of distress and affliction.

After the expiration of these two periods, two events are to occur. Whether or not these two events fall within the 70th seven is not immediately stated. One of them is the death of the Messiah and the other follows as a consequent, the destruction of Jerusalem and the Temple by the Roman armies of Titus.

For the period of the 70th seven the Messiah causes a covenant to prevail for many, and in the half of this seven by His death He causes the Jewish sacrifices and oblation to cease. His death is thus seen to belong within the 70th seven. Consequent upon this causing the sacrifices and oblation to cease is the appearance of a desolator over the pinnacle of the Temple, which has now become an abomination. Upon the ruins a determined full end pours out. This event, the destruction of the city, does not, therefore, take place within the 70 sevens, but follows as a consequent upon the cutting off of the Messiah in the 70th seven.

The question naturally arises. What marks the termination of the 70 sevens? In answer it should be noted that the text does not say a word about the termination. The *terminus ad quem* of the 69 sevens is clearly stated, namely, an anointed one, a prince. No such *terminus ad quem,* however, is given for the 70 sevens themselves. It would seem therefore, that the *terminus ad quem* was not regarded as possessing particular importance or significance. No important event is singled out as marking the termination. All schools of interpretation, therefore, are faced with the difficulty of determining what marked the close of the 70 sevens. And all schools discover this event upon the basis of considerations other than those presented in the text. The text says nothing upon the subject. Therefore, we may safely follow the text. When the 70 sevens come to a conclusion, we do not know.[4]

Ezekiel 37—39. No wonder these chapters have been a bastion for the view which perpetuates a national Israel and a Palestine per se! The language of the book of Ezekiel, acknowledged by all to be more difficult, was directed originally to a dispossessed people who needed strong encouragement. However, Professor Patrick Fairbairn, in a work called *Ezekiel's Temple,* wrote:

> It defies all attempts to bring it within the bounds of the real (earthly). . . . an inescapable obstacle to their literalism. It is an incontrovertible evidence that the prophet had something else in his eye than the masonry stone and lime erections, and was labouring with conceptions which could only find their embodiment in the high realities of God's eternal kingdom. We regard the vast extent of the sacred area as a symbol of the vast enlargement that was to be given to the kingdom of God in the times of the Messiah.[5]

While the nonearthly kingdom viewpoint is hard pressed to adapt Ezekiel's strong language to the higher and greater kingdom of the Messiah, the earthly kingdom exponents are driven even harder to the wall. First (to be absolutely literal to both the "north" and the "four corners" descriptions) they must differentiate between the Gogs and Magogs of Ezekiel and Revelation, the former before the millennium, the latter after it. Other absurd opinions are necessitated, as in the following examples in *A Premillennial Problem,* by the late Dr. J. C. L. Carson of Coleraine, Ireland:

> Mede, the learned Premillennarian, . . . is able to inform us that the earth shall not be totally consumed, as America and Australia must of necessity be preserved from the general conflagration, in order to furnish the armies of Gog and Magog. . . . I must ask my readers what they think of a system which requires for its support to imagine that the glorified saints of heaven, and the damned in hell, are all to be brought up on the new and renovated earth, under the leadership of Christ and the Devil, for the purpose of fighting a really literal and corporeal battle. . . . We are disposed to laugh at the child, but a similar case crops up in the Premillennarian system, where the learned Dr. Burnet accounts for the armies of Gog and Magog by supposing that a new race of men "will be generated from the slime of the earth, and the heat of the sun."[6]

The proper understanding of Ezekiel 37—39 is aided greatly by bearing in mind Ezekiel's perspective. The "former years" refer to the time during or *before* the Babylonian captivity; the latter years" to the time *after* it. It is of further help to remember that historically the chief battle was with Antiochus Epiphanes (Ezekiel 38—39). Chapters 40—48 are best understood as picturing the more glorious realities of the New Covenant age, couched, however, in the language of the Old Covenant people.

> . . . The basic meaning of the Book of Ezekiel will not elude the reader if he keeps in mind that God's glory and His great acts of judgment and salvation are portrayed in symbolic language and form. What Ezekiel sees in visions, describes in allegories, and acts out in a manner resembling charades, is designed to contribute to the assurance that God is carrying forward His plan of salvation for all men that He initiated in His covenant with Israel centuries ago. Purified by God's judgment in the Babylonian exile, Israel will again become the bearer of the promises to be fulfilled in the New Covenant and to the end of time. All of this Ezekiel sees in prophetic perspective, in which scenes of the immediate and of the distant future are at times superimposed on the same picture of the coming and enduring Kingdom of God.[7]

Zechariah 12—14. Zechariah's wondrous prophetic symbols, like Ezekiel's, provide fertile soil for interpretations hard to disprove.

It should be observed that, as is common in Old Testament prophecies, the details are not necessarily in chronological sequence. For instance, Zechariah 12:10 is cited by the apostle John as fulfilled Good Friday (looking on the pierced one)—not during a post-rapture tribulation period (see John 19:36-37); Zechariah 13:7 is cited by our Lord as having been fulfilled in his Gethsemane arrest the night before (see Matthew 26:31).

Whatever is made of Zechariah 14:2-3, it is clear that it speaks not of a physical millennium but of the Gospel era idealized, which issues in heaven: "There shall be neither cold nor frost. . . . there shall be continuous day . . . . living waters shall flow out from Jerusalem . . . . the Lord will become king over all the earth . . . . the whole land shall be turned into a plain . . . . But Jerusalem shall remain aloft upon its site . . . . there shall be no more curse" (Zechariah 14:6-11 RSV). This compares well with the new heavens and earth as pictured in Revelation 21—22.

A special word to those who fear to spiritualize: when the context or the literal sense would show contradiction, it is valid and safe to take something figuratively so long as it is understood to picture realities, realities which are greater. Accordingly, Zechariah 14:4 speaks of something greater than a physical split of the Mount of Olives. On the east side of Jerusalem it now rises from the valley of the Kidron to a height of some 600 feet. Zechariah 14:4 states:

> In that day His feet will stand on the Mount of Olives, which is in front of Jerusalem on the east; and the Mount of Olives will be split in its middle from east to west by a very large valley, so that half of the mountain will move toward the north an the other half toward the south.

The sensible and simple meaning of the passage is this:

> The Lord Jesus Christ has already stood upon the Mount of Olives, and from its brow He looked down upon the city which represented the Hebrew nation. That nation fell into two parts at His coming.[8]

If indeed Zechariah 14 spoke of a physical millennium, how contradictory it would be (as also when Ezekiel's prophecies are misinterpreted) to have the perfect sacrifice, our Lord Jesus Christ, be a party to the reintroduction of Old Testament sacrifices and feasts which He ended forever! These would not be memorials but insults. What grotesque follies are compounded from error.

CHAPTER 3

The Apostolic Writings on Things to Come

The apostles preached the same message to Jew and Gentile, "solemnly testifying to both Jews and Greeks of repentance toward God and faith in our Lord Jesus Christ" (Acts 20:21). The Holy Spirit dealt with both alike:

> And opening his mouth, Peter said: "I most certainly understand now that God is not one to show partiality, but in every nation the man who fears Him and does what is right, is welcome to Him. The word which He sent to the sons of Israel, preaching peace through Jesus Christ (He is Lord of all)— . . . . While Peter was still speaking these words, the Holy Spirit fell upon all those who were listening to the message. And all the circumcised believers who had come with Peter were amazed, because the gift of the Holy Spirit had been poured out upon the Gentiles also. For they were hearing them speaking with tongues and exalting God. Then Peter answered, "Surely no one can refuse the water for these to be baptized who have received the Holy Spirit just as we did, can he?" (Acts 10:34-47).

The progression of the kingdom into the church, composed of converted Gentiles and of Jews whose blindness is removed, is a fact for which there is ample Scripture testimony, for example, Acts 15:13-18 (RSV):

> . . . James replied, "Brethren, listen to me. Simeon has related how God first visited the Gentiles, to take out of them a people for His name. And with this the words of the prophets agree, as it is written, 'After this I will return, and I will rebuild the dwelling of David, which has fallen; I will rebuild its ruins, and I will set it up, that the rest of men may seek the Lord, and all the

Gentiles who are called by My name, says the Lord, who has made these things known from of old.'"

The passage just quoted has been interpreted otherwise:

Instead of identifying the period of Gentile conversion with the rebuilding of the tabernacle of David, it is carefully distinguished by the *first* (referring to Israel's coming glory.)[1]

But this misses the point, for the passage is not giving a chronological order. Gentiles are in view throughout it, the "rebuilding" being applied not to Jews but to Gentiles.

Acts 15:13-18 is a very important passage in this discussion. . . . James declares that this rebuilding of the tabernacle of David is now [was then] taking place in God's visiting the Gentiles to take out of them a people for His name.[2]

The apostles are very clear as to the fact that Jesus is reigning now.

All the apostles teach that Christ began his reign when he ascended to heaven. They will quote the prophets to prove that Jesus Christ fulfills all the predictions.[3]

Acts 2:29-31 is an example:

Brethren, I may confidently say to you regarding the patriarch David that he both died and was buried, and his tomb is with us to this day. And so, because he was a prophet, and knew that God had sworn to him with an oath *to seat one of his descendants upon his throne, he looked ahead and spoke of the resurrection of the Christ,* that he was neither abandoned to Hades, nor did His flesh suffer decay.

(The problem section of Romans 9—11 is treated in chapter 10 of this book.)

1 Corinthians 15:23-24 has been a subject of debate. Here is a helpful commentary on it:

The word "then" in the phrase "then cometh the end" does not necessarily imply an interval between the resurrection of the saints and "the end"; it is often used of immediate sequence. Many pre-millenarians admit this. Also let us notice that the

41

word 'cometh' has no equivalent in the Greek, so that the phrase is just "then the end."[4]

The following four passages are of great significance for a study of Christ's coming: 1 Thessalonians 5:1-4; 2 Thessalonians 1:6-10; 1 Peter 4:7; and 2 Peter 3:10-12. (See chapter 9 for a detailed analysis.)

The Antichrist, the Great Tribulation, and Armageddon

In approaching the final book of the Bible, it will be helpful to comment briefly on three themes that are much in prophecy discussions today: *The Antichrist, the Great Tribulation,* and *Armageddon.*

There is not much disagreement on the matter of Antichrist, once Daniel's prophecies are understood properly. (See chapter 2.) 2 Thessalonians 2 and John's epistles have never presented difficulty in the traditional understanding of prophecy. The problem arises when a view is proposed that puts Antichrist after the alleged secret rapture (taking out) of the church. God the Holy Spirit, not the church, is the restrainer of Antichrist. As to whether Antichrist is an actual person—it would seem so; however, the Antichrist is not manifested in such a way that Christians can set their watches by it. Though we are not in darkness, yet this matter and others will remain in the realm of mystery.

The Great Tribulation is this life. Our Lord has made that clear in John 16:33 and elsewhere. At the same time, He speaks of two periods when the manner of this tribulation would be unique: (1) In the destruction of Jerusalem under Titus in 70 A. D., in which, in the words of Josephus, "eleven hundred thousand," that is, 1,100,000, perished. It is reported that Titus, the Roman general, surveying the valleys below the walls of Jerusalem and seeing them full of bodies that had been cast down because of the stench, with thick putrefaction running about them, groaned, and called God to witness that this was not his doing. (2) In the time before the end, as Christian martyrs of recent history have found. The remainder of this chapter explains the structure of the Book of Revelation; chapter 14 shows why it is unwise to hold an escapist view of the great tribulation. See also a concordance for the use of the word "tribulation" in the Bible.

The Battle of Armageddon may be also a physical conflict—wars and rumors of wars, Word War III, who knows? But its greater meaning is the spiritual battle between evil and righteousness. The Book of Revelation uses Old Testament imagery of enemy nations arrayed against God's church, symbolized by Jerusalem. The *principle* is in operation. Similarly our Lord indicates that this conflict will be fiercest in the final times before His coming. This is not a premillennial coming, however, for Armageddon does not lead into a kingdom age (see Revelation 16:15-21) but rather brings a seeming end of the world. (See parallel vision charts at the end of this chapter.)

In the Book of Revelation there is no hint of a secret coming of Christ between chapters 3 and 4 or elsewhere. Other than that, chapter 20 is the main section of divergent interpretations. These are treated in chapter 5 of this book.

Repetitive Visions

The most important clue to interpreting the Book of Revelation correctly is the Holy Spirit's use of repetitive visions. It is well said in a convincing and widely used interpretive work on the last book of the Bible:

> There is, in the main, an adoption of what has been called the synchronistic or parallelistic system of interpretation. That system is (and deserves to be) gaining the approval of orthodox scholars.[5]

Said system is required *especially* when the book is interpreted more literally. In language much like that of Christ in Matthew 24:29, and of Peter in Acts 2:19-20, Revelation comes to the first of a half dozen climaxes, each of which sounds like the end of the world. It is particularly plain that repetition history is demanded by the following examples:

> I looked when He broke the sixth seal, and there was a great earthquake; and the sun became black as sackcloth made of hair, and the whole moon became like blood; and the stars of the sky

43

fell to the earth, as a fig tree casts its unripe figs when shaken by a great wind. And the sky was split apart like a cross when it is rolled up; and *every mountain and island were moved out of their places* (Revelation 6:12-14).

"*Every island* fled away, *and the mountains* were not found" (Revelation 16:20). Not to mention "the stars" falling to the earth in 6:13. The point is this: if all mountains and islands are moved out of their places in 6:14, how can they flee away, not to be found in 16:20? Parallel visions are the answer. The charts at the close of this chapter try to set forth the parallels.

An able spokesman is correct in observing:

A key issue in our understanding of the millennium is whether chapter 20 involves recapitulation, looking back from the end to the whole history of the church. In chapter 12, it is unmistakably clear that the passage looks back to the birth of Messiah. However, in the present passage, no such indication is to be found.[6]

Recapitulation does not exclude a sort of deepening and completing progression in the visions. The book builds in terror, yet God is in control and has the last word. Those who follow the view of the preceding quotation will find it needful to treat chapter 20 as recapitulation, once a reasonable comparison is made of such passages as Revelation 6:14 and 16:20.

The following charts give a general outline, though the division points are not always clear in John's visions.

If more than once, when the end is nearly reached, the writer turns back to the beginning, he does this in order to gather up new views of life which could not be embraced by a single vision.[7]

The general principle of recapitulation certainly is valid. And it gives added weight to that validity, for instance, to find a reference such as that in William Hendriksen in *More Than Conquerors,* (pp. 258—259), who lists 21 writers who assert parallelism for a proper handling of the Book of Revelation.

No answer is the full answer to such a marvelous gem as John's Revelation. Dionysius of Alexandria showed a commend-

Schematic of the Book of Revelation

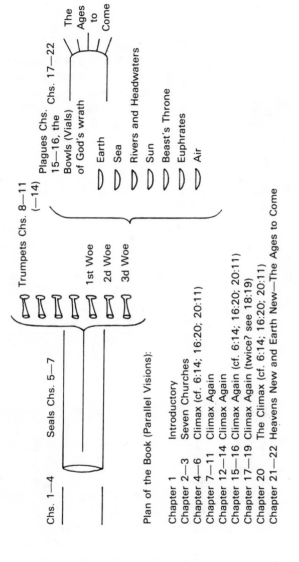

Plan of the Book (Parallel Visions):

Chapter 1 — Introductory
Chapter 2—3 — Seven Churches
Chapter 4—6 — Climax (cf. 6:14; 16:20; 20:11)
Chapter 7—11 — Climax Again
Chapter 12—14 — Climax Again
Chapter 15—16 — Climax Again (cf. 6:14; 16:20; 20:11)
Chapter 17—19 — Climax Again (twice? see 18:19)
Chapter 20 — The Climax (cf. 6:14; 16:20; 20:11)
Chapter 21—22 — Heavens New and Earth New—The Ages to Come

45

Plan of the Book of Revelation:
Parallel Visions, Synchronous
as required by such examples
as: Chapter 6:14
**   Chapter 16:20**
**   Chapter 20:11**

Ch. 1
Chs. 2—3

Vision 1 Chs. 4—6
Vision 2 Chs. 7—11
Vision 3 Chs. 12—14
Vision 4 Chs. 15—16
Vision 5 Chs. 17—19
Vision 6 Chs. 20

The Rapture
and End:
Judgment Day

New Heavens and Earth
Heaven, Hell, the
Ages to Come
Vision 7   Chs. 21—22

Book of Revelation
Parallel Visions

Inter-Advent
Period

Chapters 4—6

Chapters 7—11 (:18)

Chapters 12—14

Chapters 15—16 (:20)

Chapters 17—19 (:20)

Chapter 20

Same general history
but from various
perspectives,
or for various
purposes and
emphases.

able restraint with the Book of Revelation and its visions: "I have regarded them as too lofty to be comprehended by me."[8]

The following quotation may serve to summarize this chapter dealing with the apostolic writings on things to come.

> The well-known English Christian worker, Mr. Frank L. Carter, writes: "Having in mind the teaching of all the New Testament writings, I affirm that the notation of a future millennium is unapostolic. Paul, James, Jude, Peter and John, are silent about such a thing in their letters. Could this be so were the doctrine of the millennium a part of the Christian deposit?"[9]

Our study now moves to the church's understanding.

CHAPTER 4

How the Church Has Understood Things to Come

It is commonly assumed and said by premillennialists that the early church was premillennial. In this chapter that contention will be explored in the church fathers, creeds, the reformers, and confessional documents.

William E. Cox in a catalog of testimonies states:

> The great majority of the church fathers, reformers, commentators, and teachers of the Bible have been either amillennial or postmillennial.[1]

Even earlier, A. D. 81—96, in the closing days of the apostles, Jesus' relatives are recorded as follows:

47

There were yet living of the family of our Lord, the grandchildren of Judas, called the brother of our Lord, according to the flesh. These were reported as being of the family of David, and were brought to Domitian, by the Evocatus. For this emperor was as much alarmed at the appearance of Christ as Herod. . . . When asked also, respecting Christ and his kingdom, what was its nature, and when and where it was to appear, they replied, "that it was not a temporal nor an earthly kingdom, but celestial and angelic; that it would appear at the end of the world, when coming in glory he would judge the quick and dead, and give to every one according to his works.[2]

The Testimony of the Church Fathers

Nine church fathers of prominence are reviewed. The Australian scholar Lawrence Rowe Thomas has the following to say about the views of the fathers regarding Daniel 9 and the Book of Revelation:

An able authority, the late Rev. E. P. Cachemaille, M. A., Scholar of Gonville and Caius College, Cambridge, and Secretary of the South American Missionary Society, writes: "In the writings of the Fathers there are a multitude of references to the prophecy of Daniel and St. John. They correctly grasped the general principle that the prophets foretold the whole course of the Churches' warfare from the first century to the second advent. None of the Fathers entertained the idea of the Apocalypse overleaping the interval up to the consummation. The Judaic symbols of Daniel and St. John were generally referred to the Church and worship. Julius Afrikanius, Clement of Alexandria, Tertullian, explain the Seventy Weeks of Daniel Nine and the foretold desolations as being fully accomplished at Christ's death and the subsequent desolations of Jerusalem. So also Eusebius who spoke of the prophecy as being fulfilled years ago. So also Athanasius."

There was but one dissentient, Hippolytus. But he could never produce one text in support of his notion, hence the Fathers ignored his swansong. The modern Judaisers likewise cannot show us one Scripture.[3]

The same writer adds later:

There is no trace of a terrestrial millennial reign of Christ in the writings of Polycarp, the two Clements, Hermes, Dionysius, Ignasius, Diognius, Afrikanius, Athanasius, Cyril, Jerome and many others. The early document, The Didache, is free of millennialism also. The indices to the Ante-Nicean Fathers show 'Millennium' twice only.

Papias took his millennium fable from the uninspired book of Baruch. Justin and Barnabas based their millennium on the days of creation.[4]

Similar observations are frequent in the writings of those attempting to refute the idea of an earthly millennial kingdom. Grier states:

> In the first half of the second century there are really only two to whom we can point with any certainty as hold a future reign of Christ on earth for a thousand years—Papias and Justin Martyr. There was, of course, the heretic Cerinthus also.[5]

Eusebius, in his *Ecclesiastical History*, refers to Papias as a historian but as including

> some other matters rather too fabulous. In these he says there would be a certain millennium after the resurrecton, and that there would be a corporeal reign of Christ on this very earth; which things he appears to have imagined, as if they were authorized by the apostolic narrations, not understanding correctly those matters which they propounded mystically in their representations. For he was very limited in his comprehension, as is evident from his discourses, yet he was the cause why most of the ecclesiastical writers, urging the antiquity of the man, were carried away by a similar opinion; as, for instance, Irenaeus, or any other that adopted such sentiments.[6]

As for Justin Martyr's writings, preserved in *The Ante-Nicene Church Fathers,* they are inconsistent on the subject, as shown by comparing "The First Apology of Justin" and his "Dialogue with Trypho the Jew." At least it was a mild form of millennialism, with believers simply living in Jerusalem for 1,000 years preceding "the eternal resurrection and judgment of all men."

> Papias and Justin, then, are the only two of all the writers in the first sixty years of the second century who may with any certainty be called premillenarians....Others definitely by their

statements exclude premillenarianism. The first two volumes of the Fathers in the Ante-Nicene Library contain 950 pages, but the indices give only two references under the word 'millennium'; these two are to the statements of Papias and Justin.[7]

Let us pass from the Apostolic Fathers to the Old Catholic Church (A. D. 150—250). . . . The Apostles' Creed in its earlier forms comes to us from this time, and, according to it, there is no corporeal advent of Christ upon earth after His ascension on high, until He leaves 'from thence' to the last Judgment.[8]

The third century witnessed a very decided opposition to belief in an earthly millennium. Origen argued against it. His arguments at length gained a complete victory.[9]

Besides these, there are two works of his [Dionysius] *On the Promises*. The occasion of his writing this arose from Nepos, a bishop in Egypt, having taught, that the promises given to holy men in the Scriptures, should be understood more as the Jews understood them, and supposed that there would be a certain millennium of sensual luxury on this earth. Thinking, therefore, that he could establish his own opinion by the Revelation of John, he composed a book on this subject, with the title, *Refutation of the Allegorists*. This, therefore, was warmly opposed by Dionysius, in his work *On the Promises*.[20]

Lactansius was the only man of note in the fourth century who still held the system. Athanasius, the great defender of the doctrine of the deity of Christ against the Arians, speaks of Christ coming to judge the world; the good will then receive the heavenly kingdom and the evil will be cast into the eternal fire. This is his simple statement of the doctrine of the Lord's return.[11]

Augustine, who was one of the greatest men of the Christian Church of all time, lived A. D. 354—430. He at first adopted premillenarianism, but gave it up as "carnal." Augustine, says S. J. Case, laid the ghost of (pre-)millenarianism so effectively that for centuries the subject was practically ignored.[12]

In expounding Revelation Twenty, Augustine explained the binding of Satan as the fulfillment of the words of Jesus: "No man can enter into a strong man's house and spoil his goods unless he first binds the strong man." The reigning of the saints with Christ he looked upon as a present actuality.[13]

The Testimony of the Creeds

The Apostles' Creed in its earliest form dates from approximately A. D. 150. This and other creeds of the church uniformly look for only one return of Christ, and of the end of the world. "From thence He shall come to judge the quick and the dead" (The Apostles' Creed). To think of the kingdom of Christ as yet future contradicts the creeds of Christendom, starting with the baptismal creeds of the second century; for Christ *did* set up a kingdom, they uniformly declare, and everyone born again is now in it.

The Nicene Creed (ca. A. D. 325):

[He] ascended into heaven, and sitteth on the right hand of the Father; and He shall come again with glory to judge both the quick and the dead; whose kingdom shall have no end.

The Athanasian Creed (ca. A. D. 500):

. . . . He ascended into heaven; He sitteth on the right hand of he Father, God Almighty; from whence He shall come to judge the quick and the dead. At whose coming all men shall rise again with their bodies and shall given an account of their own works. And they that have done good shall go into life everlasting; and they that have done evil, into everlasting fire. This is the catholic faith; which except a man believe faithfully and firmly, he cannot be saved.

Such declarations are all-inclusive and show no earthly kingdom intervening between the first and the final advent.

The Testimony of the Reformers

When the Reformation came, millenarianism again appeared. It was an item in the belief of a wild and fierce sect of the Anabaptists.[14]

Luther spoke of those who were duped by the idea that before Judgment Day the Christians alone will possess the earth and that there will be no ungodly.[15]

Calvin is definitely on record as bitterly opposed to a wrong understanding of the millennium. Grier makes the following comment on Calvin's *Institutes,* Vol. 2, Book III, Chapter 25, Section 5:

Calvin shows contempt for pre-millennial ideas when he says in the chapter on "The Final Resurrection" in his *Institutes,* that Satan has endeavored to corrupt the doctrine of the resurrection of the dead by various fictions, and adds: "Not to mention that he began to oppose it in the days of Paul, not long after arose the Millenarians, who limited the reign of Christ to a thousand years. Their fiction is too puerile to require or deserve refutation." [16]

Yet many today assume that Calvin taught premillennialism. He was a foe of it!

Anyone seeking additional statements of the Reformers can find them in such works as *Documents of the Christian Church,* selected and edited by Henry Bettenson, or in Philip Schaff's *The Creeds of Christendom.*

The Testimony of the Confessional Documents

To the three ecumenical creeds (Apostles', Nicene, and Athanasian), may be added the doctrinal theology of the Eastern Orthodox Church, the Roman Catholic Church, and that of various Protestant churches. Selections from several of the latter are quoted here as representative of the array of communions that have adhered to what may be termed the traditional position on the millennium.

The Augsburg Confession (Lutheran), A. D. 1530:

> Also they (the Lutherans) teach that at the Consummation of the World Christ will appear for judgment, and will raise up all the dead; He will give to the godly and elect eternal life and everlasting joys, but ungodly men and the devils He will condemn to be tormented without end.
>
> They condemn the Anabaptists, who think that there will be an end to the punishments of condemned men and devils.
>
> They condemn also others, who are now spreading certain Jewish opinions, that before the resurrection of the dead the godly shall take possession of the kingdom of the world, the ungodly being everywhere suppressed (Article XVII).

The Belgic Confession (Reformed), A. D. 1561:

> Finally, we believe, according to the Word of God, when the time appointed by the Lord (which is unknown to all creatures) is come, and the number of the elect complete, that our Lord Jesus

Christ will come from heaven, corporally and visibly . . . (Article XXXVII).

The Westminster Confession of Faith (Church of England, Church of Scotland, Presbyterian), A. D. 1643:

At the last day, such as are found alive shall not die, but be changed; and all the dead shall be raised up with the self-same bodies, and none other, although with different qualities, which shall be united again to their souls forever. The bodies of the unjust shall, by the power of Christ, be raised to dishonour; the bodies of the just, by His Spirit, unto honor, and be made conformable to His own glorious body (Chapter XXII, II—III).

The New Hampshire Baptist Confession, A. D. 1833:

We believe that the end of the World is approaching; that at the last day Christ will descend from heaven, and raise the dead from the grave to final retribution; that a solemn separation will then take place . . . (Article XVIII).

Here is more from the Presbyterian heritage regarding the New Testament era:

In addition to our acquaintance with the Bible itself, it is profitable to consult the findings of those who have made a scholarly and exhaustive study of it. In this connection one thinks of the great Westminster Assembly of Divines, probably representing greater theological leaning than any other Assembly before or since. This momentous conclave could not find in the Word of God the things which men profess to see so plainly in our day. The Westminster Assembly linked up the Lord's return with the general resurrection and judgment, but nowhere in their conclusions can one find a place for the interjection of one thousand years of earthly bliss. Their interpretation leaves room for only the amillennial eschatological position.[17]

In May 1944 the Southern Presbyterian Church in the United States adopted a report against dispensationalism.

The general tenor of our Lord's teaching and of the entire New Testament is that one should hold fast the original doctrine and be wary of latter day departures from it. The historic church, "the pillar and ground of truth" (1 Timothy 3:15, KJV), from its beginning has dealt with every conceivable form of new interpretation. A study of the best-known articles of faith will show that Orthodox, Roman Catholic, and major Protestant groups all conclude from Scripture a return of Christ only at the end of the world.

CHAPTER 5

Revelation 20 Rightly Understood

Revelation 20 is a summary of church history.

Revelation 20:1-10, and notably verse 4, says *nothing* about Christ's coming to earth to *reign*. As pointed out in the Introduction to this book, it is a heavenly reign, not necessarily one on earth, that is meant. The language of Revelation 5:10, in fairness, should be considered in this connection. "They will reign upon the earth" need not mean corporeal reign, for the Greek word translated "upon" can just as well be rendered "over"; thus the reign could be conducted from heaven. Also it may point to the eternal reign in the new earth.

Satan Bound and Christ Reigning

The fact that it is hard to grasp that Satan is bound now makes one an easy prey to error. Revelation 20 for the most part speaks of a restraint on his *deceiving* power. Furthermore, the Greek allows for a rendering of either "any longer" or "any further" (verse 3). That is to say, Satan's work of deceiving was greatly eclipsed at the first advent of Christ. Before that time, Satan had the whole world in his grasp except for a feeble, tiny number of true believers who waited for the consolation of Israel. What a difference today!

Christ, the Light, has come into the world, and there are about a billion believers!

The two most significant passages regarding the binding of Satan are not found in the Book of Revelation. The first reads:

> Angels who did not keep their own domain, but abandoned their proper abode, He has kept in eternal bonds under darkness for the judgment of the great day (Jude 6).

Satan of course is one of those fallen angels. Note the past tense: "has kept in eternal bonds." Satan has been in bonds ever since he fell. To say that he is not bound contradicts this clear statment. The second passage is 2 Peter 2:4:

> God did not spare angels when they sinned, but cast them into hell and committed them to pits of darkness, reserved for judgment.

Note again the past tense, also the words "hell" and "pits of darkness."

That binding of Satan was effected specifically by the cross of Christ. The binding is a matter of degree. Matthew Henry gives this natural explanation of Revelation 20:2-3:

> . . . a certain term of time, in which he should have much less power and the church much more peace than before. The power of Satan was broken in part by the setting up of the gospel kingdom in the world; it was further reduced by the empire's becoming Christian.[1]

In *Pilgrim's Progress,* John Bunyan has a character give the advice, "Stay in the middle of the path, for the lions are chained."

It is difficult to understand how Satan can be bound and yet be active, but that is simply a paradox. The same word is used of the marital relationship, if that helps to understand it better.

It should be pointed out also that not all evil in the world is due to satanic activity. Man cannot say in every case, "The devil made me do it." That the devil is bound, therefore, is not to say all evil has ceased.

Though limited or restrained as on a leash, Satan is a dangerous being within the scope of activity God allows him. Therefore we are warned: "Be of sober spirit, be on the alert.

Your adversary, the devil, prowls about like a roaring lion, seeking someone to devour" (1 Peter 5:8).

Toward the end of time God gives the devil great freedom to do his worst. At such times it becomes easier to understand how even difficult times were indeed a millennium.

Ramm quotes Joseph Parker of London: "He [Satan] was chained at the first, he has been chained ever since." [2]

Victorinus, A. D. 290, wrote: "Those years wherein Satan is bound are in the first advent of Christ." [3]

The mistaken notion that Christ is not really reigning yet is likewise contrary to Scripture. In Matthew 28:18 the Lord Jesus Christ declares: "All authority has been given to Me in heaven and on earth." The prayers of the church these many centuries have ended, "For thine is the kingdom and the power and the glory forever," and Christ is addressed as the One "who lives and rules with the Father and the Holy Ghost, one God, ages without end. Amen."

It must be understood that He reigns no less if it is His will to permit evil. Satan now works out of the abyss, but he is in check.

Satan is bound and Christ is reigning, as shown in the second of the following two charts. The reader is referred also to the other charts in this chapter and in chapter 3.

The First Resurrection

There is much confusion about the first resurrection. In the dispensational system Revelation 20:4 does not coincide with the rapture, which supposedly occured seven years earlier! To get around this conundrum, Scofield, in an ingenious twist, explains:

> The "first resurrection," that "unto life," will occur at the second coming of Christ (1 Cor. 15:23), the saints of the Old Testament and church ages meeting Him in the air (1 Thess. 4:16, 17); while the martyrs of the tribulation, who also have part in the first resurrection (Rev. 20:4), are raised at the end of the great tribulation. [4]

If the rapture with its vast resurrection occurs before Revelation 20, the piece of cake is eaten and in fairness one should no longer call that later resurrection the *first*. But a

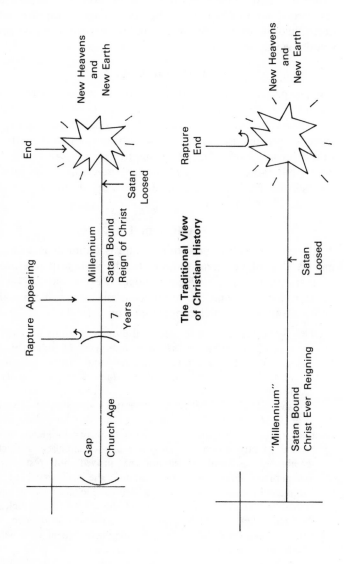

The Premillennial View of Christian History

Rapture   Appearing

Millennium

Satan Bound
Reign of Christ

End

New Heavens
and
New Earth

Satan
Loosed

7
Years

Gap

Church Age

The Traditional View of Christian History

Rapture
End

New Heavens
and
New Earth

Satan
Loosed

"Millennium"

Satan Bound
Christ Ever Reigning

57

literalist can outspiritualize anyone when convenient. At least the "pretribs" and "midtribs" too should give the round to the "posttribs" on this scorecard. But it is a faulty rapture, whether pretribulation or postribulation, unless the rapture and end are simultaneous.

Gog and Magog.

What a perfect way of stating briefly the dark days prior to His coming for the church. It is how our Lord taught. Satan is loosed, that is, given sway again. What a battle—an Armageddon indeed—spiritual for sure and perhaps accompanied with global war, who can say? Verse 9 speaks not of a 1,000-year kingdom saints, but rather of God's children ("the camp of the saints and the beloved city") whether in John's day or in ours, if we are living at Christ's return.

Judgment Day.

A greater subject than the millennium is found in Revelation 20, namely that of the great judgment. Any system of interpretation is a spiritual tragedy which removes Revelation 20:11-15 as a concern for everyone. A premillenarian with a more balanced approach makes a good commentary on verse 11:

> This is the preparation for the final judgment. Some interpreters are greatly interested in the time and place of judgment and theorize that there are several different and distinct judgments taught in the New Testament: the judgment of the nations to decide which nations enter the millennial kingdom (Matt. 25:31-40); the judgment of believers before the judgment seat of Christ in heaven to receive their rewards for what they have done in the body (2 Cor. 5:10); and the great white throne judgment of the present passage which is a judgment only of unbelievers. Such a scheme of eschatology cannot be proved but rests upon unsupported inferences. For instance, the final issue of the judgment of nations is not the millennial kingdom but is either eternal life or eternal punishment (Matt. 25:46). This is clearly the final judgment which decides the eternal destiny of men. The judgment seat of Christ is also the judgment seat of God before which all believers must stand (Rom. 14:10). Scripture is not primarily interested in what concerns many students of the Bible,

viz., in a scheme or chronology of prophetic events, and such efforts to differentiate between several different judgments do not have sound biblical support. However, the fact of judgment is solidly rooted in biblical thought. Paul affirms it unequivocally (Rom. 2:6-10).[5]

The following charts are included as clarifications of the Book of Revelation, especially of chapter 20. The second uses terms that vary among millenarian systems: the rapture, the appearing, and the end—these may be designated also as the rapture, the revelation, and the consummation.

In summary, the millennium is Christ's inter-advent period of restraint on Satan until a final, brief release. "Thousand" often means completeness in the Bible. The *1,000 years* hint at an extended period. Strange that those who futurize it and can stretch the *day* the Lord or even an *hour* (John 5:28-29) into 1,007 years and more, nevertheless demand that the 1,000 years of Revelation 20 must mean just that, and in a book of so much symbolism! Inconsistency, thou art the rule.

The Book of Revelation
in the Traditional View

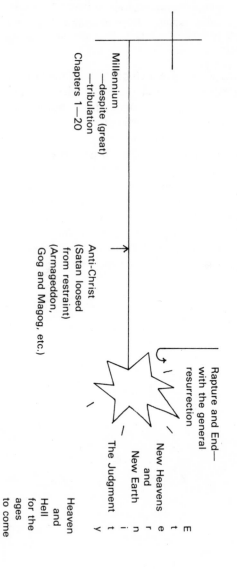

Millennium
—despite (great)
—tribulation
Chapters 1—20

Anti-Christ
(Satan loosed
from restraint)
(Armageddon,
Gog and Magog, etc.)

Rapture and End—
with the general
resurrection

New Heavens
and
New Earth

The Judgment

Eternity

Heaven
and
Hell
for the
ages
to come

The Book of Revelation
in the Premillennial View

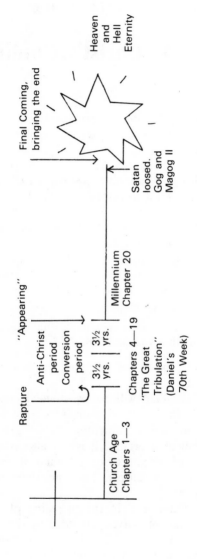

Rapture

"Appearing"

Anti-Christ
period
Conversion
period

3½
yrs.

3½
yrs.

Final Coming,
bringing the end

Heaven
and
Hell
Eternity

Millennium
Chapter 20

Satan
loosed.
Gog and
Magog II

Chapters 4—19
"The Great
Tribulation"
(Daniel's
70th Week)

Church Age
Chapters 1—3

CHAPTER 6

At Christ's Coming

Will His coming be quiet and invisible? Will the world continue after His coming? Will He return again to reign on earth for 1,000 years?

The foregoing chapters have presented general answers. Now, more specifically, what will happen when Christ comes?

It will be helpful to review what leads up to this momentous event.

Outwardly, things will continue about as at present. The general signs spoken of by our Lord will become more intensified, but this has been happening and is almost imperceptible. Our Lord points to this situation in explaining that it will be business as usual, so to speak. There will be a general unawareness of the end; it will be unexpected.

> For this reason you be ready too; for the Son of Man is coming
> at an hour when you do not think He will (Matthew 24:44).

Meanwhile, the church will continue bearing witness to Christ until He comes.

Marked apostasy will be in vogue increasingly as the end approaches. This will culminate in the emergence of the personification called Antichrist. It is generally believed the Antichrist will be a person. It is not altogether clear whether he will arise out of the church or move into it from without. But the Antichrist will be a usurper. These are times of great trial for the people of God.

Then in a moment, in the twinkling of an eye, Christ will come with clouds of heaven, attended by the holy angels and the saved who are now with Him. The resurrection will occur in that same moment as the saved soul is reunited with its gloriously resurrected body. These rise first to meet the Lord in the air, while also those believers living on earth will be transformed in body, changed, and will be caught up together with the sainted dead to meet the Lord in the air.

As this happens, the earth and universe will disintegrate with awesome destruction which those who are left must pass through as they are brought to judgment. In this same dissolution of the universe, a destruction by explosive fire, there will occur also the refashioning which God has promised, resulting in the new heavens and new earth as the abode of righteousness.

In the same act of resurrection spoken of above, Christ will raise also the unsaved dead. Each soul presently in the preliminary hell will be reunited also with its raised body, but it will be a body of shame and contempt. Indescribable anguish that will never end begins for these, for whom all hope is lost. As in Dante's epic, the entrance to the place of the damned is posted with the solemn reminder:

"All hope abandon, ye who enter here!"

The great judgment now follows in this all-encompassing event, with the fixing of eternal destinies. The lost will be cast into hell "where their worm does not die, and the fire is not quenched" (Mark 9:48). The saved will be welcomed to the new and glorious realms prepared for those who love God.

There is no place in all this for an earthly millennium after His coming. Yet the Scofield Bible footnotes speak of

> . . . the good news that God purposes to set up on the earth, in fulfillment of the Davidic Covenant (2 Sam. 7:16, and refs.), a kingdom, political, spiritual, Israelitish, universal, over which God's Son, David's heir, shall be King, and which shall be, for one thousand years, the manifestation of the righteousness of God in human affairs. . . . (p. 1343).
>
> The Dispensation of the Kingdom (2 Sam. 7:16, refs.) begins with the return of Christ to the earth, runs through the "thousand years" of His earth-rule, and ends when He has delivered up the kingdom to the Father (1 Cor. 15:24, *note*).[1]

It is this temporal "on the earth" aspect under present conditions that is in question. Will the kingdom emerge on the earth previous to the earth's destruction and refashioning? It is, to be sure, widely held that the kingdom "will finally be manifested, the consummation of all things visible on earth, the most splendid period of its history."[2] The issue is stated clearly as follows:

> Will the coming of Christ terminate this present gospel age and be followed by the last judgment and the final state? Or, will it usher in another dispensation, the millennium, during which Christ will reign on earth and after which He will come to judge the world?[3]

A scholar and minister who once embraced and taught the dispensational view of things to come but now repudiates it, has written a counteracting description of what happens at Christ's return as eternity is ushered in—

> We believe that the Second Coming of Christ will mark the end of this age and the beginning of the eternal one; We believe that the modern theory of a Secret Coming of our Lord, a Secret-Rapture of His Church, seven years before His Second Coming is a dangerous error and thoroughly unscriptural; We believe that there is but one future, bodily return of Christ, called His Second Coming, at which time the Church is Raptured; We believe that Christ's Second Coming will be as sudden and as unannounced as that of a thief in the night; We believe that at Christ's Coming the door of Salvation will be forever closed to sinners; We believe that on the day of His Coming, on the Last Day of time, at the time of harvest, our Divine, Lord Jesus Christ, our Great Prophet, Priest and King, shall descend from heaven corporally and visibly, in clouds of glory with a shout and with the voice of an Archangel, at which time there will be a General Resurrection of all the dead, of the just and that of the unjust; We believe that the righteous dead (whose bodies will have been reunited with their souls which will return from Heaven with their Lord) will rise first, and the living saints whose bodies will be suddenly changed (glorified), will be caught up together with them to meet the Lord in the air; We believe that Death will be destroyed at Christ's Coming; We believe that Christ is Coming the Second time to judge the living and the dead; We believe that at this General Judgment all apostate angels and all persons that have lived upon the earth shall appear at the Great White Throne Judgment to be judged by the most holy and righteous Judge—

our Lord Jesus Christ; We believe that on that Day everyone, both believers and unbelievers, shall be judged according to their thoughts, words and deeds, and shall be rewarded according to the deeds done in their body, whether good or evil; We believe at that Day He shall say to the wicked, "Depart from me, ye cursed, into everlasting fire, prepared for the Devil and his angels"; We believe at that Day He shall say to the righteous, "Come, ye blessed of My Father, inherit the Kingdom prepared for you from the foundation of the world"; We believe in a place of eternal torment for the damned, and an eternal Kingdom of Glory for the redeemed; We believe that at Christ's Second Advent, according to Saint Peter (2 Pet. 3:10-14), the present heavens shall pass away with a great noise, and the elements shall melt with fervent heat, the earth also and the works that are therein shall be burned up; We believe that the teaching of God's Word is very clear as to the end of the world, and we, with Saint Peter and the Church of the ages, look, at the close of this age, for a "New Heaven and a New Earth, wherein dwelleth righteousness," not for a future thousand-year age of sin and imperfection mingled with righteousness (as do all Premillennialists), a Millennial age which is supposed to consummate with the most fearful rebellion against God since man's creation.[4]

The same writer lists seven important events that will take place when Jesus comes:

1. Christ's coming shall mark the end of Christ's present mediatorial reign at God's right hand. Psalm 110:1; 1 Cor. 15:23-25.

2. Christ's coming will mark the end of the day of Salvation, of every sinner's chance to be saved. 2 Cor. 6:2; Phil 1:6; Matt. 25:10; Luke 13:25-28; 17:26-30; Matt. 13:37-43; 2 Thess. 1:7-10.

3. Christ's coming will bring the rapture of the Church, but destruction to the sinner. 1 Cor. 15:51, 52; 1 Thess. 4:16, 17; Luke 17:26-30; 2 Thess. 1:7-10; 2 Peter 3:7, 10, 11.

4. Christ's coming will bring the end of time—the end of this world. Matt. 13:37-43.

5. Christ's coming will bring the general resurrection of all men, and it will destroy death. Acts 24:15, John 5:28, 29; Rev. 1:7; John 6:39, 40, 44, 54; John 11:24; Matt. 12:41; 1 Cor. 15:25, 54, 55.

6. Christ's coming will bring the General Judgment of all mankind. Acts 17:31, 32; Matt. 16:27; Rev. 22: 12; 2 Cor. 5:10, 11; Matt. 12:36; Luke 11:31, 32; Matt. 13:24, 30, 39-43; Matt. 25:31-46; Rev. 20:11-15.

7. Christ's coming will bring destruction to the present "heaven and earth," and will bring about a "new heaven and a new earth." Matt. 24:35; Heb. 1:10-12; 2 Pet. 3:7-15; 1 Cor. 13:10; 2 Pet. 3:18.[5]

There can be no doubt whatever about the *what* of the end. But the *when* is an important question also. The story is told that a Scottish teacher of the Gospel once asked a group of young ministerial students if they thought the Lord might come that very day. Each was asked in turn, and each answered in turn in this manner, "I think not." Whereupon the questioner said, "In such an hour as you think not, the Son of Man cometh."

CHAPTER 7

Second Chance: Error of Errors

" . . . and the door was shut" (Matthew 25:10). The main point of Jesus' parable of the Ten Virgins is preparedness; its main lesson is that if one is unprepared at His coming it will be forever too late.

Only the boldest of the bold would dare to say that this parable applies mostly to a select period and people. The reader is referred to chapter 1 of this book for discussion regarding the error of differentiating between a "kingdom of God (Gentile)" and a "kingdom of heaven (Jews)."

Any system which contradicts this *shut door principle* and which allows for even one conversion after the rapture has to be wrong and should be avoided as a fatal disease. This principle has even been held with proper fear and no doubt kept many from embracing millennial systems which do violence to our Lord's repeated warnings against any idea of a second chance. But, as has been pointed out: "One of the worst features in the teaching of many pre-millenarians is a second chance."[1] It hurts to find those words confirmed in writings of good and godly Christians.

> To be sure, the chiliasts teach that there will be men and women saved after the gospel dispensation, just as there were people saved before the gospel age. . . . the Church will be complete when Christ returns, but, although no more will be added to the body of Christ, many more will be added to the multitude of the redeemed of God. . . . God's Word will be found on earth after the departure of the Church for heaven.[2]

By *second chance* in this discussion is not meant a repeated offer but an extension of the day of salvation. Christ spoke of returning only once at the end of the world. Therefore all systems must be scrapped which keep the door of salvation open after His one and only coming to judge the living and the dead. Gross error may sound reasonable:

> The revising editor of the Scofield Bible, Mr. E. Shuyler English, wrote us: "Nowhere does the Scofield Bible teach a second chance. If I read my Bible aright, when Christ arrives He shall find many who had never heard the true Gospel and will then do so. This is not a second chance but a first chance."[3]

But *today* is the day of salvation. There will be no other.

A widely heard radio Bible teacher stated that the greatest moving of the Spirit of God will be after the church is taken away! Some premillennial teachers soften this objectionable aspect by saying that only Jews will have a second chance for salvation after Christ comes for the church; some say that Jews and certain Gentiles will have a second chance; still others make the second chance a wholesale opportunity with multitudes that no man can number being saved after Christ's return for the church. And really this latter view is more consistent with premillennialism for otherwise there could not be the spiritual and other millennial perfections.

In line with this, Ironside, a noted Bible teacher of the past, gives the view echoed by so many today. His lecture on Revelation 7:13-14 reads:

> It seems very strange that some have taught that in this great multitude we have the raptured church; hence they have supposed that the Lord would not come for His church until the middle of the tribulation period; but a careful study of the passage makes it very evident, it seems to me, that we are here gazing upon an earthly, not a heavenly, company. This great multitude embraces the Gentile nations who will enter into millennial blessing. It is *the great ingathering* of the *coming* dispensation, when from all nations, and kindreds, and peoples, and tongues, a vast throng from all parts of the earth will be redeemed to God by the blood of the Lamb, and will enter into the earthly kingdom of our Lord. During the dark days of the great tribulation they will heed the testimony which will be carried to the ends of the earth by Jewish missionaries . . . "[4]

Many disturbing manifestations of this falsehood are cropping up. Books on how to be saved if one misses the rapture and how to survive during the tribulation are being marketed.

Songs such as, "I Wish We'd All Been Ready" and "The King Is Coming" tend to sow this dangerous idea of more time after Christ's coming—an open door to second chance teaching.

A 14-year-old reportedly told his preacher father something like this: "Dad, I'm not going to accept the Lord now. But I promise you if I miss the rapture, I will accept Him even if I have to have my head cut off."

Bulletin boards announce rapture topics such as, "Resurrection—Don't Miss It."

A Bible lecturer on a university campus advised a large audience that if they should miss the rapture, each should fall down on his knees immediately because the great tribulation would be coming.

Bumper stickers pass along the idea: One reads: "In case of the RAPTURE this car will be unmanned."

At a local supermarket the writer one day was standing in a checker's line. The checker knew that the writer was a Gospel minister. Leaving the line momentarily, unnoticed by her, he picked up a forgotten item. Coming back he saw that she looked like death warmed over. "Oh!" she gasped, "Oh! I thought I missed the rapture!"

Damaging films are being shown such as "Thief in the Night." It concocts a story of a young couple—he is saved and so disappears at the rapture, but she is left. Refusing to join the 666 peace coalition, she at last commits suicide. Audience applause was unreal, appalling—a sort of erroneous western. One is left to wonder, was she saved by suicide? If not, she should have played it cool for three and a half years so as to get in on the mass conversion supposedly coming. The film was ostensibly based on 1 Thessalonians 5:1-3:

> Now as to the times and the epochs, brethren, you have no need of anything to be written to you. For you yourselves know full well that the day of the Lord will come just like a thief in the night. While they are saying, "Peace and safety!" then destruction will come upon them suddenly like birth pangs upon a woman with child; and they shall not escape.

But in the film's false doctrinal system, there *was* no destruction, no end. Moreover they *did* escape.

Offered now for unsaved loved ones are guides for survival after the church is gone, instructions for those who are left. With denominational approval, a 2,000-member church in southern California has changed its bylaws to provide continued leadership if its officers suddenly are taken to heaven. Error compounds. In still another example, an effort has been launched to stockpile Bibles in hidden, protective capsules for those who are left on earth after the rapture so that they may make it yet as "tribulation" saints.

A community in Illinois (Steele) is preparing to survive the tribulation.

Satan loves, furthers, and prospers any doctrine which hints to people that there may be a second chance. Such an assurance fosters a wait-and-see attitude.

This false teaching is bound to work great harm in the future. The pages of Christian history contain many such examples. Years ago a great stir was caused by an erroneous expectation of the rapture. Newspapers were ready, just in case, with a headline that could be set on the presses in twenty minutes: "MILLIONS DISAPPEAR." When nothing happened, a credibility gap followed. It was a great victory for the devil. It confused some believers who turned away. It turned off much of the church from an interest in prophecy. It caused people in general to ignore Christianity. There is a great danger of that again!

CHAPTER 8

More than One Return, Resurrection, Judgment?

Will there be plural returns, plural resurrections, plural judgments? That depends on whether the day of the Lord will occur in stages or will be one climactic, simultaneous event.

> The common New Testament teaching does not give us two, three, or even four resurrections. The New Testament speaks again and again of the resurrection of just and unjust in one breath. It speaks of the Lord's coming bringing blessing to His own, and at the very same time 'destruction' to the ungodly.[1]

The order of the last events is as follows: Christ's return simultaneous with the end; judgment issuing into hell and heaven; the ages to come.

Regarding our Lord's return, the Bible teaches that it will occur in the same manner as that of His departure; that is, He will come on the clouds of heaven with power and great glory. At least seven different Scripture passages from Daniel to Revelation affirm that He is coming with clouds and that every eye will see Him. (Daniel 7:13; Matthew 24:30-31; Luke 21:27; Mark 14:62;

Acts 1:11; Revelation 1:7; 14:14). By the miracle of an instantaneous resurrection and the momentary destruction of the heavens and the earth, people in all ages and lands, from Adam to the last person born, shall see His coming. In the face of this clear Scriptural teaching, how can one believe that Christ will first come secretly for the church and that the world will continue for 1,007 years plus a little season after that, before His visible coming at the time of the end? 1 and 2 Peter, for example, show that the apostle looked only for this one, final return of Christ and that he expected it and the end of all things to occur simultaneously. Christ's coming brings the end. 1 Peter points not to a secret coming of Christ but to "the end of all things" (1 Peter 4:7). In 2 Peter this is made even more plain. That day is *not* going to occur in stages (the rapture, then Christ's appearing, then the end):

> In the last days mockers will come . . . saying, "Where is the promise of His coming? For ever since the fathers fell asleep, all continues just as it was from the beginning of creation." (2 Peter 3:3-4)

> The day of the Lord will come like a thief, in which the heavens will pass away with a roar and the elements will be destroyed with intense heat, and the earth and its works will be burned up (2 Peter 3:10).

At His return the church is to be "raptured" or caught away. 1 Thessalonians 4:16-17 speaks of how the church is to be caught up, caught away into bliss. Our Lord Jesus Christ, speaking of the end, explains how the times will be like those of Noah, days of intense wickedness and defiance toward God.

> Then there shall be two men in the field; one will be taken, and one will be left. Two women will be grinding at the mill; one will be taken, and one will be left. Therefore be on the alert, for you do not know which day your Lord is coming (Matthew 24:40-42).

The expressions "taken" and "left" may seem to suggest that the world goes on despite Christ's coming. But they need not have that meaning. They simply reveal that at Christ's coming human beings will be separated, the saved taken and the lost left. Left with the world continuing? The answer must be no, according to Scripture, including 1 Thessalonians 4:13-18. This passage simply states that those not taken are left to pass through the awesome destruction of the earth and will be brought into the Judgment.

That Judgment is one and the same with (1) the so-called Christian judgment of works (1 Corinthians 3:15), and (2) the alleged premillennial judgment of the nations (Matthew 25:31-46).

Regarding (1) above, the Christian hope is not confidence that one will *escape* Judgment Day but confidence *for* it (see 1 John 4:17). Jesus does not teach in John 5:24 that the Christian goes unjudged. Judged, yes; condemned, no. The following Scriptures are clear. 2 Corinthians 5:10: "We must all appear before the judgment seat of Christ, that each one may be recompensed for his deeds in the body, according to what he has done, whether good or bad"; Romans 14:10, 12: " . . . we shall all stand before the judgment seat of God. . . . each of us shall give account of himself to God"; Matthew 16:27: God "will . . . recompense every man according to his deeds." When one adds to these the "every word" and "every deed" passages (Matthew 12:36; Ecclesiastes 11:9; 12:14), the most that could be hoped for on the basis of other Scriptures is that only the things confessed and forgiven will go unremembered on that day.

Regarding (2) above, the outcome of Matthew 25:31-46 is not a millennium but hell or heaven, and that for *all* the nations of history. This is the Judgment of Revelation 20—the Judgment before the great white throne. All *judgment* has been committed to the Son (John 5:22), though obviously the *judgment seat* of Christ and of God are the same.

Augustus Strong, one of the most eminent Baptist theologians and teachers of his day, disagreed with the two-resurrection, premillennial system which, he said, "we are combatting."[2]

The other Scriptures contain nothing with regard to a resurrection of the righteous which is widely separated in time from that of the wicked, but rather declare distinctly that the second coming of Christ is immediately connected both with the resurrection of the just and the unjust and with the general judgment.[3]

It is not right to teach that the Judgment need not concern the Christian because he will be elsewhere, having been judged 1,000 years earlier (and only for work rewards). No one will escape the Judgment. The teaching of Scripture on the subject of Judgment Day should awe the best of men.

CHAPTER 9

The Rapture and the End Are Simultaneous

Not two events but one—the saved are caught away as the world ends. This has been the understanding of the vast majority from the beginning. They find no difficulty in so believing. They have no hang-ups with prophecy; where a literal earthly interpretation would be contradictory and senseless, they understand it naturally as transcendent reality. Thus an earthly reign is out of the question. Further, both Testaments, Old and New, speak of but one climactic event, the great assize and transition, in which saved and lost participate. The flood is set forth as the example of this by Christ and by Peter.

Four principal passages now must end all doubt.

After all it is only just for God to repay with affliction those who afflict you, and to give relief to you who are afflicted and to us as well when the Lord Jesus shall be revealed from heaven with His mighty angels in flaming fire, dealing out retribution to those who do not know God and to those who do not obey the gospel of our Lord Jesus. And these will pay the penalty of eternal destruction, away from the presence of the Lord and from the glory of His power, when He comes to be glorified in His saints on that day, and to be marveled at among all who have believed—for our testimony to you was believed (2 Thessalonians 1:6-10).

A passage such as the above could not be more plain in showing that there is but one coming or appearing or return of Christ and that this is accompanied simultaneously with the destruction and renovation of the heavens and the earth. It is evident that Paul is comforting the Thessalonians with the thought of Christ's possible coming then (with deliverance and destruction) and not 1,000 years later. But the premillennialists must interpret this passage as speaking of a later coming, for obviously if there is to be an earthly millennium, the earth cannot be destroyed at the rapture. Therefore the end of the world in this view is always no less than 1,000 years away. The passage under discussion is so plainly contrary to that idea, however, that its meaning must be twisted. It is explained that a period should be placed before the word "when," so as to allow an interpolation: "When the Lord Jesus [after the millennium] shall be revealed from heaven . . . ." But this changes the original meaning and intent which was to comfort the suffering Christians at Thessalonica with the hope that the Savior might come soon, bring retribution to their tormentors and relief to themselves, a double-edged event. The premillennialist interpretation of the passage is wrong grammatically. Regardless, God forbids such twisting of His words. Still, dispensationalism everywhere inserts these 1,000-year separations and pluralizings.

> The day of the Lord will come like a thief, in which the heavens will pass away with a roar and the elements will be destroyed with intense heat, and the earth and its works will be burned up. Since all these things are to be destroyed in this way, what sort of people ought you to be in holy conduct and godliness, looking for and hastening the coming of the day of God, on account of which the heavens will be destroyed by burning, and the elements will melt with intense heat! (2 Peter 3:10-12)

This is a passage that is almost untwistable. Peter's readers are admonished to be "looking for and hastening" His coming (see 2 Peter 3:4) which, clearly, will bring simultaneous destruction. To get around this, some maintain that Peter simply was not well enough informed about the day of the Lord, namely that a millennial kingdom must first run its course after Christ's coming. So the "day of the Lord" is interpreted as a stretched-out period. This does not, however, alter in the slightest degree the plain words of this chief apostle who had heard Christ's kingdom explanations over a period of 40 days (Acts 1:3). He too had raised the question of Acts 1:6 about the restoration of the kingdom to Israel. (The reader may wish to refer to chapter 1 of this book for a discussion of that question.) Here an informed Peter says nothing about an earthly kingdom to follow Christ's return.

> Now as to the times and the epochs, brethren, you have no need of anything to be written to you. For you yourselves know full well that the day of the Lord will come just like a thief in the night. While they are saying, "Peace and safety!" then destruction will come upon them suddenly like birth pangs upon a woman with child; and they shall not escape. But you, brethren, are not in darkness, that the day should overtake you like a thief (1 Thessalonians 5:1-4).

Paul's teaching here is just as clear as Peter's in showing that these Thessalonians might possibly experience the unexpected and sudden day of the Lord, which would come like a thief bringing destruction, not a mere disappearance of Christians. Paul and Peter both use the "thief" concept. This does not mean a quiet coming, but only an unexpected coming. When it comes, the heavens will pass away with a roar and the elements will be destroyed with intense heat, and the earth and its works will be burned up" (2 Peter 3:10).

> The end of all things is at hand; therefore, be of sound judgment and sober spirit for the purpose of prayer (1 Peter 4:7).

Here is another troublesome passage for those who hold an earthly kingdom view. Such a view certainly would contradict Peter's words, having him say, in effect, that the beginning of a Golden Age for the earth was at hand. "The end of all things" does not suggest a world intact after the rapture occurs.

Speaking of the rapture as simultaneous with the end, George Murray writes:

It has been the age-old belief of the Christian Church that God has, in His own eternal councils, appointed a day in which He shall bring the members of the human race before His judgment seat to be assigned to their eternal destinies. This belief is amply supported by the Holy Scriptures which speak of the Lord's return, the resurrection of the dead, and the final judgment, as simultaneous events. This is also suggested by the Apostles' Creed which speaks of Christ's return, and the judgment of the quick and the dead, in the same clause. In Scripture, and elsewhere, the time when this series of events shall take place is described as "the day of the Lord," or "the day of Christ."

How much difference does it make, one might ask, whether a person looks for Christ's coming as the end or simply as the rapture? It makes a great deal of difference, as an Irish Presbyterian points out:

> Let no one say that all this discussion matters little. The idea of the wicked being summoned to the bar of God more than a thousand years later than the righteous, tends, to say the least, to lessen 'the terror of the Lord', a terror which the Scriptures again and again seem to associate with His coming at the last trump for the great and universal assize.[2]

The same observation can be made regarding whether one looks for a secret, silent event as about to happen, or something worse than nuclear holocaust! The "tone" of one's faith is affected or, one could say, infected by the outlook. All such softening and postponing take the edge off the urgent prophecy.

There is tremendous convicting power in the proper teaching of Christ's coming as simultaneously bringing universal destruction. Spurgeon, in a sermon entitled "The World on Fire," captures the tone:

> Am I ready to be caught away to be with my Lord in the air? Or shall I be left to perish amidst the conflagration? How ought I live! How ought I to stand as it were on tip-toe, ready when He shall call me, to be away up into the glory, for off from this perishing world![3]

Here is his invitation at the close of the sermon:

> I would to God that all here present were prepared for the future.

You remember John Bunyan makes Christian sit in the City of Destruction at ease until he hears from one called Evangelist, that the city was to be burned up, and then he cries, "Alas, alas, woe is me, and I shall be destroyed in it." That thought set him running, and nothing could stop him. His wife bade him come back, but he said, "The city is to be destroyed, and I must away." His children clung about his garments to hold him, but he said "No, I must run to the City of Safety, for this city is to be burned up." Man, it will all go! If all your love is here below, it will all go! Your gold and silver will all go! Will you not have Christ? Will you not have a Savior? For if you will not, there remains for you only a fearful looking for of judgment and of fiery indignation. Tempt not the anger of God. Yield to his mercy now. Believe in His dear Son. I pray that you may this day be saved, and God be glorified in your salvation. Amen.[4]

CHAPTER 10

Israel and Israeli

"Only a remnant of them will be saved" (Romans 9:27 RSV)— "All Israel will be saved" (Romans 11:26 RSV). There is no contradiction in these statements if they are understood correctly.

There are five meanings of "Israel" in the Bible: (1) the 12 tribes; (2) the northern 10 tribes; (3) Jews (Israel according to the flesh); (4) spiritual Israel (true Jewish believers); (5) the Israel of God (the saved, both Gentiles and Jews).

The following passages show clearly that it is a mistaken view to perpetuate the Old Testament usage of "Israel." Romans 2:28-29; 4:16-17; Galatians 3:28-39; 6:15-16; Ephesians 2:12-13; 3:6. This eliminates the first two meanings above.

Read as a unit, Romans 9—11 does not lead one to conclude

that God is planning a Palestinian kingdom and a mass conversion of Jews after Christ comes. First, one should read Romans 9:1-3. These verses tell of Paul's great sorrow over the unbelief of his people according to the flesh. If it were true that conversion en masse and a glorious earthly kingdom were ahead for them, his tears were foolish. The only hope he held out for them was that the inclusion of Gentiles as the Israel of God would provoke them to repent and turn to their Messiah, as many of them have done.

Paul's inspired line of reasoning in Romans 9—11 is to praise the depth of God's riches and wisdom and knowledge, and His unfathomable ways. Nearly all Jews might have been lost, but a certain hardening in Jewry led the apostles to turn to the Gentiles (recall Acts). The inclusion of *Gentiles* as children of Abraham (Romans 9:7-8) was to make the Jews jealous (Romans 11:11, 13-14, 31), causing a remnant of them to be saved. Thus God had never rejected His people whom He foreknew (Romans 11:1-2, 5), nor has His Word failed (Romans 9:6). So in this manner *all* Israel (the true Israel of God, composed of saved Gentiles and saved Jews) will be (is being) saved. How tremendous of God!

Romans 11:26-27 speaks of Christ's *first* advent exclusively, when He came once for all to take away sins. To place this in the future is another gospel not taught in Scripture.

When all the evidence is brought in, one must have the courage to say finally that even if this passage could seem to be taken either way, the one must be chosen which is in harmony with the rest of Scripture. Nothing is to be added to or taken away from Scripture in order to accommodate a scheme that allows for salvation after Christ returns.

As to the times of the Gentiles, Scripture in speaking of Jerusalem as "trampled under foot by the Gentiles until the time of the Gentiles be fulfilled" (Luke 21:24), does not by the word "until" necessarily indicate that anything is to follow except Christ's coming at the end of history. This event is not followed by restoration and millennium but leads into the end.

The prophecy stands today remarkably fulfilled even after nearly 30 years of the modern nation called Israel. Jerusalem continues a mixed population, with Gentile influence remaining—

a Muhammadan temple, the Mosque of Omar, stands on the site of the ancient Jewish temple.

That site, Mt. Zion, will not be raised physically higher than the Himalaya mountains (Mt. Everest is five and a half miles high) for a millennial reign of Christ from there. Prophecies along those lines speak simply of our greater present Gospel era in contrast to the former Old Testament era. Superior to all existing philosophies, the Gospel has been attracting all nations, as the Lord indicated, from his first advent onward, drawing all to Himself.

What will happen to the land of Palestine when the world ends? Like the rest of the world, it will be destroyed, then refashioned. Its tenants will have to move out at least temporarily. The promise that Israel was not to be dislodged again would be contradictory unless it is applied to the greater New Covenant concept of Israel of God and to the heavenly inheritance (1 Chronicles 17:9). It is well said, "Israel's inheritance is the new earth."

What is the significance of the reestablishment of a national Israel in 1948? It does not herald a millennial kingdom. It may be a sign fulfilling Matthew 24:34 which means possibly that the *Jewish* generation would remain identifiable as a people till the end of time. But the question has been raised whether modern "Jews" are true Jews. The prophecy must be handled with caution and restraint. Could it be that the wrong application of this prophecy is a part of the great deception by which even the very elect are in danger of being deceived?

There have been other notable returns to Palestine. Modern Israel points out that throughout the centuries Jews have returned to the land individually and in groups, and that almost every century has seen waves of immigration to the land. Edward Gibbon notes in *The History of the Decline and Fall of the Roman Empire* that such a return was granted under Julian (emperor 361—363); in it the Jews began to rebuild the temple. He speaks of respectable evidence to the effect that strange occurrences such as an earthquake, whirlwind, and a fiery eruption prevented and finally ended the effort. Some Christian writers claim that a luminous cross appeared in the heavens. A similar return had taken place about A. D. 125 under Trajan. So checkered history has continued for that oppressed people. St. Paul points out in Romans 11:28 that as regards the election, they are beloved on account of the fathers. However, as a learned Bible teacher said, not the Jewish people but Jesus Christ is the timepiece of prophecy.

Palestine and Israel—Christian Arabs—Christian Jews—confusing? It need not be. God loves all. He does not want His people of old or others mistreated but wants them to find true rest in this world. Yet he has a better homeland prepared for everyone who turns to Jesus the one Messiah for mankind. Above all, he wants Jew and Gentile to gain the heavenly Jerusalem.

CHAPTER 11

A Critique of
The Late Great Planet Earth

There is always a danger in taking something out of context, but at times this is necessary in order to focus on specifics rather than on overall impact. The method of this chapter will be to list first all the quotations to be considered, then follow with a section of running commentary.

Following are brief excerpts from the book, *The Late Great Planet Earth*, by Hal Lindsey and C. C. Carlson. These are cited of course within the "all rights reserved" guidelines and limitations.

> One portrait of the Messiah depicts Him as a humble servant who would suffer for others and be rejected by His own countrymen. . . . The other portrait shows the Messiah as a

conquering king with unlimited power, who comes suddenly to earth at the height of a global war and saves men from self-destruction. He places the Israelites who believe in Him as the spiritual and secular leaders of the world and brings in an age free of prejudice and injustice.[1]

The general time of this seven-year period could not begin until the Jewish people re-established their nation in their ancient homeland of Palestine.

(Keys to the Prophetic Puzzle) A definite international realignment of nations into four spheres of political power had to occur in the same era as this rebirth of Israel. Each sphere of power had to be led by a certain predicted nation and allied with certain other nations. The relationships of all these factors to each other is easily determined by the following clues: first, each one of the four spheres of political power is said to be present and vitally involved with the reborn state of Israel.

Secondly, each one of these spheres of power is a major factor in the final great war called "Armageddon," which is to be triggered by an invasion of the new state of Israel.

Third, each one of these spheres of power will be judged and destroyed for invading the new state of Israel, by the personal return of the Jewish Messiah, Jesus Christ.

. . . .

The one event which many Bible students in the past overlooked was this paramount prophetic sign: Israel had to be a nation again in the land of its forefathers.[2]

. . . a careful distinction must be made between "the physical restoration" to the land of Palestine as a nation, which clearly occurs shortly before the Messiah's coming and the "spiritual restoration" of all Jews who have believed in the Messiah just after His return to this earth. . . . the great catastrophic events which are to happen to this nation during "the tribulation" are primarily designed to shock the people into believing in their true Messiah (Ezekiel 38:39).[3]

The fact that the Jews had to be restored as a nation before Christ could return was seen by James Grant, an English Bible scholar writing in 1866.

"The personal coming of Christ, to establish His millennial reign on earth, will not take place *until the Jews are restored to their own land,* and the enemies of Christ and the Jews have gathered together their armies from all parts of the world, and have commenced the siege of Jerusalem . . . now the return of the Jews to the Holy Land, and the mustering and marshalling of these mighty armies, with a view to capturing Jerusalem, must require a *considerable time yet*."[4]

Jesus said that this would indicate that He was "at the door," ready to return. Then He said, "Truly I say to you, *this generation* will not pass away until all these things take place" (Matthew 24:34 NASB).

What generation? Obviously, in context, the generation that would see the signs—chief among them the rebirth of Israel. A generation in the Bible is something like forty years. If this is a correct deduction, then within forty years or so of 1948, all these things could take place. Many scholars have studied Bible prophecy all their lives believe that this is so.

Obstacle or no obstacle, it is certain that the Temple will be rebuilt. Prophecy demands it.[6]

Watch the actions of Iran in relation to Russia and the United Arab Republic. This writer believes that significant things will soon be happening there.[7]

The attack upon the Russian confederacy and the resulting conflict will escalate into the last war of the world, involving all nations. Then it will happen. Christ will return to prevent the annihilation of all mankind.[8]

. . . (Isaiah 19:4 RSV). This refers to the Anti-christ of Rome who will possess Egypt after Russia is destroyed.[9]

One sentence in that story leaped from the page: "Should all go according to the most optimistic schedules, the Common Market could someday expand into a ten-nation economic entity whose industrial might would far surpass that of the Soviet Union."[10]

When it says that the beast will emerge out of the sea, it means that he will come out of the chaos of the nations.[11]

[The Antichrist] . . . you may be asking, "How can this possibly happen while Christians are in the world?" . . . It cannot.[12]

It is logical to ask at this point, how is he going to make war with the saints when they are gone from the earth? "The saints" are the people who are going to believe in Christ during this great period of conflict. After the Christians are gone, God is going to reveal Himself in a special way to 144,000 physical, literal Jews who are going to believe with a vengeance that Jesus is the Messiah. They are going to be 144,000 Billy Grahams turned loose on this earth—the earth will never know a period of evangelism like this period. These Jewish people are going to make up for lost time. They are going to have the greatest number of converts in all history. Revelation 7:9-14 says they bring so many to Christ that they cannot be numbered.[13]

Those who remain on earth at that time will use every invention of the human mind to explain the sudden disappearance of millions of people.[14]

"There I was, driving down the freeway and all of a sudden the place went crazy . . . cars going in all directions . . . and not one of them had a driver. I mean it was wild! I think we have got an invasion from outer space! . . . You really want to know what I think? I think all that talk about the Rapture and going to meet Jesus Christ in the air was not crazy after all. I don't know about you, brother, but I am going to find myself a Bible and read all those verses my wife underlined."[15]

The big question is, will you be here during this seven-year countdown.[16]

The distinction between God's dealing with the church and His dealing with another group of believers who are largely gathered around Israel is very important. . . . we distinguish between the second advent, or the second coming of Christ, and the Rapture.[17]

Christians sometimes have a theological debate about whether the Rapture occurs at the same time as the second coming of Christ or whether it takes place before the second coming, even before the Tribulation. It is only fair to sincere Christians who differ about this time element for us to develop the reasons why we believe the Bible distinguishes between the Rapture and the second coming of Christ and why they do not occur simultaneously. . . . During the Tribulation the spotlight is on the Jew—in the Book of Revelation, the Jew is responsible for evangelizing the world again (Revelation 7:14).[18]

However, in the Rapture, only the Christians see Him. . . . When the living believers are taken out, the world is going to be mystified.

. . . .

Here is the chief reason why we believe the Rapture occurs before the Tribulation: the prophets have said that God will set up a kingdom on earth over which the Messiah will rule.

. . . .

We need to understand that during the seven-year Tribulation there will be people who will become believers at that time.

. . . .

The largest descriptive volume of the Tribulation is found in Revelation 6 through 19.[19]

It is clear that the U.S. cannot be the leader of the West in the future.[20]

As Armageddon begins with the invasion of Israel by the Arabs and the Russian confederacy, and their consequent swift destruction, the greatest period of Jewish conversion to their true Messiah will begin.

. . . .

Zechariah predicts that one-third of the Jews alive during this period will be converted to Christ and miraculously preserved.[21]

The clouds then would be all of the church age believers, you and I, returning in immortal glorified bodies, having been previously caught up to meet Christ in the air in "the ultimate trip" prior to the seven years of Tribulation on earth, and the resurrected saints of the Old Testament. (Revelation 19:14).[22]

Jesus' feet will first touch the earth where they left the earth, on the Mount of Olives. The mountain will split in two with a great earthquake the instant that Jesus' foot touches it.[23]

We are "premillennialists" in viewpoint. The real issue between the amillennial and the premillennial viewpoints is whether prophecy should be interpreted literally or allegorically.[24]

It is promised that Jerusalem will be the spiritual center of the entire world and that all people of the earth will come annually to worship Jesus who will rule there (Zechariah 14:16-21; Isaiah 2:3; Micah 4:1-3).[25]

Keep your eyes on the Middle East. If this is the time that we believe it is, this area will become a constant source of tension for all the world. The fear of another Word War will be almost completely centered in the troubles of this area. It will become so severe that only Christ or the Antichrist can solve it. Of course the world will choose the Antichrist.

Israel will become fantastically wealthy and influential in the future. Keep your eyes upon the development of riches in the Dead Sea.

The United States will not hold its present position of leadership in the western world; financially, the future leader will be Western Europe.[26]

Comments.

It is unfortunate that the commendable portions of that book cannot be treated.

There is much value in some of its literal applications. There *is* a last generation, and the present one may be it! But to teach absolutely that this one must be it is a serious error.

> People whose hopes are often incited to expect the fulfillment of what they accept as prophecy are equally disappointed when their hopes do not materialize. The result is that some lose faith in the Scriptures, rather than in those who undertake to interpret them.[27]

The viewpoint that Christ will intervene with peace[28] is completely foreign to anything He Himself has said. It holds out a false hope to the unsaved world. The only thing Christ ever promised was one coming that will bring eternal bliss to His followers and eternal woe to unbelievers.

Regarding the Palestine question,[29] see chapter 10.

The interpretation of "this generation" (Matthew 24:34) given by Lindsey and Carlson is one of some seven possible interpretations. This view leads to the danger of saying that Christ must return within one generation counting from A. D. 1948, when the nation of Israel was established. Some count a generation to be 20 years, but since 1968 came and went without incident, 1988 is the new limit. That sort of thing has been tried before. It would be well if Hegel's point ("History teaches us that man learns nothing from history"), used as a caption for Lindsey and Carlson's third chapter, page 27, were applied also to the above date-setting.

As for the conjecture made on page 97 (regarding the Common Market nations), all things are possible, of course, especially in prophetic interpretation.

Note the spiritualizing in the quote from page 104. Revelation 17:15 is interpreted symbolically. Strange that some cannot see other symbolism in the Bible.

The saddest part of the whole book and the most dangerous is the second-chance teaching of pages 111, 167, and 177, namely, the supposed mass conversion of Jews and the "144,000 Jewish Billy Grahams," who supposedly will win "the greatest number of converts in all history" *after* Christ's coming. This is the worst feature of dispensational premillennialism, and directly contradicts Christ and His repeated solemn warnings against any such thought or hope.

Pages 135, 136, 142, and 143 (see quoted references) contain more error. The reader is referred to chapters 7 and 9 of this book for comments on the damage done by second-chance teaching and nonsimultaneous rapture and end teaching.

In some countries it would be considered subversive to make statements such as the samples excerpted from pages 161 and 184 of Lindsey and Carlson's book. If the United States falls from leadership it will not be because of prophecy.

> The New Testament simply does not contain any predictions which apply to certain specific present-day nations or states, to these and to these only. It describes the struggle between the church and the world. It says nothing that refers exclusively or even specifically to China, Japan, the Netherlands, or Louisiana![30]

Indeed, citizens thinking America is doomed to that fate may help bring it about. How wrong and how foolish! Is oft-quoted 2 Chronicles 7:14 no longer in the Bible? Someone once commented that, if one man held off the destruction of Sodom and Gomorrah, there is hope of preservation through the prayers of America's millions upon millions of Christians.

The crass literalism of page 174 can but give a heavy heart to those who know that the prophecy involved points to something far greater than the physical.

Page 184 is more commentary than prophecy. No one could prove a person wrong about the volatile Middle East situation. But if it does not turn out as Lindsey and Carlson project, and the Lord further delays His coming, and if the Jews were to lose Palestine to the Arabs or Russia in a cat and mouse game, what then? A concerned radio listener had sent in that conjecture. The otherwise fine and capable speaker answered something like this, "That won't happen. That's can't happen." He proceeded to explain as if Scripture so teaches.

These observations against some Christians make the heart sad. But they need to be made. This is not to say, however, that the critic is a better Christian. One regrets having to speak critically regarding soul winners.

This writer heartily agrees with the following: "We should plan our lives as though we will be here our full life expectancy, but live as though Christ may come today."[31]

CHAPTER 12

The Handwriting of the Heavens

It is a great spiritual tragedy of our times, this writer feels, that a large segment of the evangelical church has been taught to understand the Bible dispensationally. This is tragic for a number of reasons, not least of which is the failure to use the impact of the space age to advantage.

An explanation is in order. It is this. Unless one looks for the end of the world rather than a secret coming of Christ, one will not rightly feel the full apocalyptic impact of the nuclear age. The edge is taken off imperceptibly. Moreover, in such a case, that note not only is diminished in one's own perception, but he fails to project it in his witness.

The language of our Lord was unmistakable. He spoke of the end of the world, never of a secret rapture. This approach by the Son of God is well calculated and should be much employed in the present hour. But that impact is blunted in the thinking and tone of those who do not look for the end as at hand since it is always, in their view, at least 1,000 years away, as stated in chapter 9.

Astronomy is this writer's hobby. One vivid impression it makes is that the massive destruction of the heavens and earth spoken of in the Bible is happening constantly on a smaller scale throughout the universe as a star here or there becomes a super nova, i.e., explodes, and in that moment disintegrates vast areas. Should the star we call our sun do that, our entire solar system would be obliterated in a moment, in the twinkling of an eye, by an indescribable explosive burst.

Our present knowledge of the universe and a right understanding of Biblical teaching have moved closer, not farther apart. The Bible never taught that the earth is flat or that the universe is three-storied. From its holy and revealing pages men might have guessed that the earth is not static but in motion and that the universe is composed of orbiting bodies. The Word of God is always more up-to-date than scientific knowledge which at best trails far behind. Further disclosures of God's creative witness may be expected as time and discovery continue, God granting.

Some utterances of God's Word have become intelligible only in our time, such as: the circle of the earth (Isaiah 40:22), earth reeling to and fro like a drunkard (Isaiah 24:20), courses (Judges 5:20), risings and circuits (Psalm 19:6), and the like. Job 26:7 states, "He . . . hangs the earth on nothing." Concepts such as eternity itself, the bottomless pit, perpetual fire, end of the world physically—these make sense. Thus the concept of everlasting hellfire means that very thing, not just a burning conscience that people fearlessly have even now.

Creation's witness in this space age is greater than ever. Psalm 19:1 says it pointedly to the 20th century:

> The heavens are telling of the glory of God;
> And their expanse is declaring the work of His hands.

Here inspired David thinks of all of God's vast creation, particularly of the heavenly bodies—the stars, our sun and moon, and of the firmament or atmosphere that surrounds us.

In other psalms, simply, yet majestically, he sings the praises of our great Creator as he regards the wonders of the earth and the marvel that he is "fearfully and wonderfully made" (Psalm 139:14).

Truly nature is one vast, effective sermon; and never more so than in a scientific age. Someone has referred to sun, moon, and stars as God's "traveling preachers." Joseph Addison put it splendidly:

The spacious firmament on high,
With all the blue ethereal sky,
And spangled heavens, a shining frame,
Their great Original proclaim.
The unwearied sun from day to day
Does his Creator's power display,
And publishes to every land
The works of an almighty hand.

Soon as the evening shades prevail
The moon takes up the wondrous tale,
And nightly to the listening earth
Repeats the story of her birth;
Whilst all the stars that round her burn,
And all the planets in their turn,
Confirm the tidings as they roll,
And spread the truth from pole to pole.

What though in solemn silence all
Move round the dark terrestrial ball;
What though nor real voice nor sound
Amid their radiant orbs be found;
In reason's ear they all rejoice,
And utter forth a glorious voice,
Forever singing as they shine,
"The hand that made us is divine."

The heavens declare not only the existence of God but also His *glory*. How do they do this? By showing order, power, beauty; by hinting of eternity; by displaying God's patience, faithfulness, mercy, love, destructive power; His wisdom, His inexhaustibleness—the list grows long.

The witness of nature is powerful. "Declare" and "proclaim" are forceful words. The manifold works of nature point to God as their source. In wisdom He made them all. His painstaking care is seen in everything.

O Lord, our Lord
How majestic is Thy name in all the earth,
Who hast displayed Thy splendor above the heavens!
From the mouth of infants and nursing babes
Thou hast established strength,

Because of Thine adversaries,
To make the enemy and the revengeful cease.

When I consider Thy heavens, the work of Thy fingers,
The moon and the stars, which Thou hast ordained;
What is man, that Thou dost take thought of him?
And the son of man, that Thou dost care for him?
Yet Thou hast made him a little lower than God,
And dost crown him with glory and majesty! (Psalm 8:1-5)

Much still remains unknown. It is a deception to think that a full disclosure of all the truth waits just around the corner. The years ahead will bring greater witness to the truth of God's Word as well as denials more bold and blind than ever. Someone has asked:

I have a life in Christ to live;
I have a death in Christ to die;
And must I wait till science give
All doubts a full reply?

It should be remembered that God will not judge us on the basis of what science says for or against Him, but on what *He* says.

There never was, nor is there today, any real excuse for unbelief. The Bible states, "Ever since the creation of the world His invisible nature, namely, his eternal power and deity, has been clearly perceived in the things that have been made. So they are without excuse" (Romans 1:20 RSV). It is neither intelligent nor reasonable to deny God's existence.

The fool has said in his heart, "There is no God."
They are corrupt, they have committed abominable deeds;
There is no one who does good.
The Lord has looked down from heaven upon the sons
of men,
To see if there are any who understand,
Who seek after God.
They have all turned aside; together they have become
corrupt;
There is no one who does good, not even one.

Do all the workers of wickedness not know
Who eat up my people as they eat bread,
And do not call upon the Lord? (Psalm 14:1-4)

90

This wretched state of man's unbelief came about as follows:

> For the wrath of God is revealed from heaven against all ungodliness and unrighteousness of men, who suppress the truth in unrighteousness because that which is known about God is evident within them; for God made it evident to them. For since the creation of the world His invisible attributes, His eternal power and divine nature, have been clearly seen, being understood through what has been made, so that they are without excuse. For even though they knew God, they did not honor Him as God, or give thanks; but they became futile in their speculations, and their foolish heart was darkened. Professing to be wise, they became fools . . . (Romans 1:18-22).

And now the situation is aggravated as described in Psalm 10:4: "The wicked, in the haughtiness of his countenance, does not seek Him."

Therefore Christians living in the space age must be decided and fervent witnesses, and should be knowledgeable. But wonderful as it is to know that God the Son is "upholding the universe by His word of power" (Hebrews 1:3 RSV), it is more wonderful still to know Him as Savior. A story is told of an atheist in London who tried to embarrass an unlettered man who had been converted. "Do you know anything about Christ?" he asked. "Yes, by the grace of God, I do," was the answer. "When was He born?" The ignorant saint gave an incorrect answer. "How old was He when He died?" Again the answer was incorrect. The atheist said with a sneer, "See, you do not know so much about Jesus after all, do you?" "I know all too little," was the modest reply, "but I know this: I was one of the worst drunkards in London. My wife was a brokenhearted woman; my children were afraid of me. Today I have one of the happiest homes in London. Jesus has done this for me. This I know."

The Christian heritage in this space age is awesome. It is to be a pressing reminder that "unto whomsoever much is given, of him shall be much required" (Luke 12:48 KJV).

Greater light—greater responsibility! The persuaded of planet earth must endeavor in love by life and word to persuade other earth dwellers.

In a day of much denial there is need for renewed affirmation. Not only must one insist on the virgin birth and physical resurrection of Christ, but also on His bodily return and the physical end of the world—the literal transformation to the new heavens and new earth. Those who treat the very end of the world figuratively must reckon with our Lord's pledge that the heavens will suffer the end as well (Matthew 24:35). Christ teaches that the end is being physically forecast by signs in sun and moon and stars, by world-wide earthquakes (studies show increasing frequency and possibly magnitude) and famine, by sea and waves roaring, and by the signs of the times themselves.

Our churches should be overflowing, "all the more, as you see the day drawing near" (Hebrews 10:25).

CHAPTER 13

The Unknowable in Things to Come

A Jesuit pointed out that there have always been two errors regarding the Lord's return: having Him come too soon or too far away.

There is a paradox in Scripture regarding the unknowable extent of Christ's kingdom. On the one hand, Christ could have come at any time; on the other, it is indicated that the extent of the kingdom is unlimited.

The glorious expectation held out in such passages as Isaiah 2, with all nations streaming to the Lord, and knowledge of the Lord covering the earth, with all knowing Him, from the least to the greatest, must be balanced with more sobering statements. The Lord spoke of the wide gate, at which many go in to destruction, and the narrow way to life, which few find. The disciples knew what He had said about going into all the world and about His possible or seeming delay in returning. They had learned the parables on readiness and hintings of delay. They went forth with the message, not knowing how many they could reach until He returned. They certainly did not think that He could not return until they reached everyone. Peter, John, Jude, and James, the Lord's brother, not to mention Paul and the writer of Hebrews, whether Paul or another, *all* expected the Lord's return. This is very significant. They knew His teaching better than we. They knew the Old Testament and how the great covenant blessings were to be understood. Peter was sharp on these matters. He saw by inspiration that Christ was on David's throne by virtue of the resurrection (Acts 2:30-31). He knew the extent of the Abrahamic covenant. Yet he looked for Christ's return as a very real possibility in his day—in terms of destruction and refashioning.

Neither the parables hinting of Christ's possible delay nor these suggesting possibly a greater extent of outreach kept them from looking for His return in their lifetime. Peter looked for it—2 Peter 3 and 1 Peter 4:7. John looked for it—1 John 2:18, 28 and 3:2, not to mention references throughout the Book of Revelation. Jude looked for it—Jude 17-18, 21. James, the Lord's brother, looked for it— James 5:7-9. Paul looked for it—1 Cor. 15:51-57; Philippians 4:5; 1 Thessalonians 3:13; 4:13-18; 5:1-4; 2 Thessalonians 1:6-10; 2 Timothy 4:1; Titus 2:13. Hebrews sees "the day drawing near (10:25)."

The chief problem perhaps is the statement of Matthew 24:14: "This Gospel of the kingdom shall be preached in the whole world for a witness to all the nations, and then the end shall come."

This does not mean that every individual must hear, much less be saved. It means the nations as a whole will have opportunity given to them and that there will be those out of every nation among the redeemed (Rev. 7:9).[1]

It is a greater error than dispensationalism if we press this worldwide extent meaning too far. Archbishop Richard Trench most wisely said, "The Second Advent is possible any day, impossible no day."

In Romans 16:26, the apostle Paul states that the Gospel of Jesus Christ "has been made known to all nations" and in Colossians 1:23, he speaks of the Gospel as having been "proclaimed in all creation under heaven." And they hoped to see His return.

The following is an interesting commentary on this question of the extent of Christ's Kingdom.

> The question is often asked—Will the world become better or worse towards the coming of the Lord? There are passages in the Bible which seem to teach very clearly that the world at His coming will be a very wicked place like the world of Noah's Day or of Lot's day (e.g., Matt. 24:37-42). And there are other passages which seem to set forth a gradual development of Christ's kingdom (e.g., Matt. 13:31-33). Both pictures are, no doubt, true. As R. B. Kuiper says: "Broadly speaking, conditions on earth are becoming better and worse at once. Witness the Christianization of pagan nations and the slipping back of Christian people into paganism." It is likely that "as the reign of the truth will be gradually extended, so the power of evil will gather force towards the end."[2]

CHAPTER 14

Safeguards for Things to Come

It is bad to teach that He must come now.

It is worse to teach that He cannot come yet.

It is worst of all to teach that He will not be coming back.

The following facts should keep one safe from the first danger named above (dispensationalism):

1) No salvation after Christ's return
2) The rapture and the end are simultaneous
3) The binding of Satan is not future
4) Christ is reigning now
5) An earthly millennium contradicts Christ, creeds, and all the Bible
6) Supposedly millennial Old Testament passages speak of "for

ever" conditions

7) Old Testament Israel has been replaced

As for teaching that He cannot come yet, the Savior's own words are the best safeguard.

As for any who think He will not be back, because they think there will be no end, let it be remembered that we live in a real universe which had a real and momentary beginning. Is it not reasonable also from a scientific standpoint to reckon with the real possibility that it will end in the same manner? Then too, for those who turn the whole Bible into one vast allegory, it should be borne in mind that symbols in the Bible mean more than they say, not less.

George Murray said it well: "We take second place to no one in our conviction that the Lord will return personally and visibly."[1]

With prophecy it should be borne in mind that spiritual realities may have earthly accompaniments. It may well be, for example, that the beasts of Revelation 13 will find their ultimate, deepest, and final fulfillment in a coalition of communism and an apostatized church, by and large. It may well be that Armageddon may turn out to be both a spiritual and physical war of global dimensions at the last, triggered in the Middle East. Who knows? No one but God. Even these dark times may not yet exhaust God's longsuffering. Further deliverance may come and the final advent of Christ not yet arrive.

Signs are indeed all around us. There *is* some significance to today's headlines. Our salvation is nearer every day, as the Word of God points out. There is an intensifying and deepening; and of course one generation *will* be the last.

Meanwhile it is wise that no one be wise in his own conceits. It should not be surprising to find true believers at opposite poles in matters of end-time prophecy. Recall Calvinism and Arminianism, both systems based on Scripture. This is not to say that nothing is conclusive, but it should provide an escape valve for those locked into schools of interpretation which prove to be erroneous. Segmented interpretation is a danger, but equally so is the kind of totality stance that is impervious to events of the day.

It is devoutly to be wished that some sort of synthesis be found of postmillennialism, premillennialism, and amillennialism. All three have difficulties, and points of agreement, complementing one another. All three end in a transcendent kingdom, real and eternal, of finer substance and conditions that will endure for eternity. The Christian community should be made aware, at least, that there are alternative viewpoints held by Bible believers who look for the transition of the heavens and earth and to enjoyment of God's kingdom forevermore.

The argument really is not between the literal and the spiritual, but between the earthly and the transcendent, both of which are literal. It is well to remember, as stated above, that earthly symbols do not mean less but more. That principle guards against either restricting the meaning of figurative language or robbing it of reality.

The writer is willing to furnish samples and suggestions for conducting seminars on "Things to Come for Planet Earth." He invites the reader to make inquiry, urging that true prophetic interpretation be sought diligently in this time of stress. That this is essential is demonstrated in something Corrie ten Boom is saying. She has been referred to as a great-aunt to all the saints, having herself graced a Nazi prison camp, and to the Orient and Europe—on both sides of the Iron Curtain. She has been quoted in many sources as follows:

> There are some among us teaching there will be no tribulation, that the Christians will be able to escape all this. These are the false teachers Jesus was warning us to expect in the latter days. Most of them have little knowledge of what is already going on across the world.
>
> I have been in countries where the saints are already suffering terrible persecution. In China the Christians were told, "Don't worry, before the tribulation comes, you will be translated— raptured." Then came a terrible persecution. Millions of Christians were tortured to death. Later I heard a Bishop from China say, sadly, "We have failed. We should have made the people strong for persecution rather than telling them Jesus would come first."
>
> Turning to me he said, "You still have time. Tell the people how to be strong in times of persecution, how to stand when the tribulation comes—to stand and not faint."

What if the midnight knock comes before the midnight shout?

That is to say, what if the secret police come before the Bridegroom comes? Dare anyone be absolutely certain it will not be, and teach men so?

Things *are* coming for planet earth. Each needs to know these matters rightly. The best assurance to be found is that *He* is coming. Each must face the very personal questions: Am I ready? Am I correctly and sufficiently informed? Am I equipped for any eventuality?

Where do we go from here? Up, of course, whether we live or die. Thanks be to God! It is the Christian's constant encouragement that "the coming of the Lord is at hand" (James 5:8).

Bibliography

Allis, Oswald T. *Prophecy and the Church.* Nutley, New Jersey: Presbyterian and Reformed Publishing Co., 1945.

Boettner, Loraine. *The Millennium.* Philadelphia: Presbyterian and Reformed Publishing Co., 1958.

Bright, John. *The Kingdom of God: The Biblical Concept and Its Meaning for the Church.* Nashville: Abingdon Press, 1953.

Cox, William E. *Biblical Studies in Final Things.* Nutley, New Jersey: Presbyterian and Reformed Publishing Co., 1964.

_____. *The Millennium.* Nutley, New Jersey: Presbyterian and Reformed Publishing Co., 1964.

Erdman, Charles R. *The Book of Ezekiel.* Princeton, New Jersey: Fleming H. Revell Company, 1956.

Eusebius. *Ecclesiastical History.* London: Samuel Bagster and Sons, 1847.

Feinberg, Charles L. *Premillennialism or Amillennialism.* Wheaton, Illinois: Van Kampen Press, 1954.

Grier, W. J. *Momentous Event.* London: The Banner of Truth Trust, 1945. This excellent, attractive paperback, by an Irish Presbyterian, sets forth the Scriptural, creedal and historic voice of the church on the final advent, which views the millennium as this extended inter-advent period of restraint on Satan before his final, unhindered onslaught.

Hanson, Robert S. *The Future of the Great Planet Earth.* Minneapolis, Minnesota: Augsburg Publishing House, 1972.

Hendriksen, William. *More than Conquerors.* Grand Rapids, Michigan: Baker Book House, 1967, 1st ed. 1939.

    To quote the book jacket, "It is not without reason that the demand for *More than Conquerors* has been so great that the publisher has been called upon to issue this twentieth printing."

Henry, Matthew. *Matthew Henry's Commentary,* Vol. VI. New York: Fleming H. Revell Company, [n.d.].

Holman, A. J. *Holman Study Bible—Revised Standard Version.* Philadelphia: A. J. Holman and Company, 1962.

Ironside, H. A. *Lectures on the Revelation.* New York: Loizeaux Brothers, 1920.

Ladd, George Eldon. *A Commentary on the Revelation of John.* Grand Rapids, Michigan: Wm. B. Eerdmans Publishing Co., 1972.

Lindsey, Hal and C. C. Carlson. *The Late Great Planet Earth.* Grand Rapids, Michigan: Zondervan Publishing House, 1970.

Lowry, Cecil John. *Christians Believe.* Oakland, California: Trinity Book Room, [n.d.].

    ——————. *Christian Catechism.* Oakland, California: Color Art Press, 1961.

Luther, Martin. *D. Martin Luthers Werke,* vol. 47. Weimar: Hermann Boehlaus Nachfolger, 1912.

McClain, Alva J. *Daniel's Prophecy of the Seventy Weeks.* Grand Rapids, Michigan: Zondervan Publishing House, 1940.

Murray, George L. *Millennial Studies.* Grand Rapids, Michigan: Baker Book House, 1948.

New American Standard Bible. The Lockman Foundation, La Habra, Calif., and A. J. Holman Co., Philadelphia, 1975;

Patton, William. *The Judgment of Jerusalem.* New York: Robert Carter and Brothers, 1877.

Pentecost, J. Dwight. *Things to Come.* Grand Rapids, Michigan: Zondervan Publishing House, 1958; rpt.

Ramm, Bernard. *Protestant Biblical Interpretation.* Grand Rapids, Michigan: Baker Book House, 1970.

Reu, M. *Lutheran Dogmatics.* Columbus, Ohio: Wartburg Press, 1951.

Sauer, Erich. *The Triumph of the Crucified: A Survey of Historical Revelation in the New Testament,* trans. G. H. Lang. Grand Rapids, Michigan: Wm. B. Eerdmans Publishing Co., 1957.

Scofield, C. I., ed. *The Scofield Reference Bible.* New York: Oxford University Press, 1909.

The Septuagint Version of the Old Testament. New York: Harper & Brothers, [n.d.].

Spence, J. D. M., and Exell, Joseph S., eds. *The Pulpit Commentary,* Vol. XII. Grand Rapids, Michigan: William B. Eerdmans Publishing Co., 1950.

Spurgeon, Charles Haddon. *The Treasury of the Bible,* New Testament, Vol. IV. Grand Rapids, Michigan: Zondervan Publishing House, 1962.

Strong, Augustus Hopkins. *Outlines of Systematic Theology.* Philadelphia: American Baptist Publication Society, 1908.

Swete, Henry Barclay. *The Apocalypse of St. John.* Grand Rapids, Michigan: Wm. B. Eerdmans Publishing Co., 1951.

Thomas, Lawrence Rowe. *Does the Bible Teach Millennialism?* Swengel, Pa.: Reiner Publications [n.d.].

Young, Edward J. *The Prophecy of Daniel.* Grand Rapids, Michigan: William B. Eerdmans Publishing Co., 1949.

Notes

Introduction

1. All Bible quotations are from the *New American Standard Bible* unless otherwise indicated.

2. Pentecost, p. 372.

3. Boettner, p. 158.

4. Reu, p. 484.

5. Cox, *The Millennium,* p. 6.

7. Ibid., p. 15.

7. Ibid., pp. 6—7.

Chapter 1

1. *Clavis Bibliorum* (1675), p. 10, cited by C. A. Briggs, *Biblical Study,* p. 363, quoted by Ramm, pp. 267—268.

2. Cox, *Biblical Studies in Final Things,* p. 39.

3. Feinberg, p. 126.

4. Cox, *The Millennium,* p. 57.

5. "A completely futuristic view of the kingdom (that in no sense does the kingdom now exist) and a completely spiritualized view of the kingdom (that the kingdom is solely the rule of God in the heart) are not true to the doctrinal teaching of the parables" (Ramm, p. 286).

6. Murray, p. 62. "The claim of modern dispensationalism is that Jesus Christ came to establish a Jewish kingdom upon the earth."

7. Allis, p. 83.

8. Scofield, p. 1027.

9. Allis, p. 75.

10. Grier, p. 61.

11. Scofield, p. 1026.

12. Ramm, p. 253.

13. Patton, pp. 59—60.

14. Eusebius, pp. 104—105.
15. Lowry, *Christian Catechism,* p. 60.
16. Thomas, pp. 8—9.
17. Lowry, *Christian Catechism,* p. 62.
18. Allis, p. 312.

19. Thomas, pp. 3—4.

20. Murray, pp. 71—72.

21. Thomas, p. 8.

22. Ibid., p. 5.

Chapter 2

1. Bright, p. 86.

2. McClain, p. 13.

3. See Young, pp. 21—22.

4. Young, pp. 220—221.

5. Thomas, p. 97.

6. Thomas, p. 98.

7. A. J. Holman, *Holman Study Bible—Revised Standard Version* (Philadelphia: A. J. Holman and Company, 1962), p. 783b. Similar explanations are offered by others as follows: J. D. M. Spence and Joseph S. Exall, eds., *The Pulpit Commentary,* XII (Grand Rapids, Mich.: Wm. B. Eerdmans Publishing Company, 1950), p. xxxiii: "Whether . . . it ought to be concluded that the prophet anticipated a final ingathering of the Jews to Palestine, with Christ reigning as their Prince in Jerusalem, it would hardly be safe to affirm . . . ."; Charles R. Erdman, *The Book of Ezekiel* (Princeton, New Jersey: Fleming H. Revell Company, 1956), p. 124: "These future glories chapter 40—48 were sketched by the prophet in figures."
8. Grier, p. 56.

Chapter 3

1. Pentecost, p. 110.

2. Grier, p. 46.
3. Thomas, p. 9.
4. Grier, p. 74.
5. Hendriksen, p. 7.
6. Ladd, p. 261.
7. Swete, p. xliii.
8. Eusebius, p. 307.
9. Thomas, p. 16.

Chapter 4

1. Cox, *The Millennium,*p. 40.
2. Eusebius, pp. 120—121.
3. Thomas, p. 25.
4. Ibid., p. 92.
5. Grier, p. 24.
6. Eusebius, pp. 143—144.
7. Grier, p. 25.
8. Ibid.
9. Ibid., p. 27.
10. Eusebius, p. 305.
11. Grier, p. 27.
12. Ibid., p. 28.
13. Ibid., p. 29.
14. Ibid.
15. Weimar ed., vol. 47, p. 561.
16. Grier, p. 30.
17. Murray, p. 15.

Chapter 5

1. Henry, p. 1179.
2. Ramm, p. xv.
3. *The Ante-Nicene Fathers,* VII, 358.
4. Scofield, p. 1228.
5. Ladd, p. 271.

Chapter 6

1. Scofield, p. 1341.
2. Sauer, p. 152.
3. Allis, p. 2.

4. Lowry, *Christians Believe*, pp. 20—22.
5. Lowry, *Christian Catechism*, p. 64.

Chapter 7

1. Grier, p. 62.
2. Feinberg, pp. 174—175.
3. Thomas, p. 74.
4. Ironside, pp. 128—129.

Chapter 8

1. Grier, p. 15.
2. Strong, p. 264.
3. Strong, p. 263.

Chapter 9

1. Murray, p. 131.
2. Grier, p. 66.
3. Spurgeon, p. 463.
4. Ibid., p. 464.

Chapter 11

1. Lindsey and Carlson, p. 29.
2. Ibid., pp. 42—43.
3. Ibid., p. 48.
4. Ibid., pp. 49—50.
5. Ibid., p. 54.
6. Ibid., p. 56.
7. Ibid., p. 68.
8. Ibid., p. 71.
9. Ibid., p. 79.
10. Ibid., p. 97.
11. Ibid., p. 104.
12. Ibid., p. 110.
13. Ibid., p. 111.
14. Ibid., p. 135.
15. Ibid., p. 136.
16. Ibid., p. 137.
17. Ibid., p. 139.
18. Ibid., p. 142.
19. Ibid., p. 143.

20. Ibid., p. 161.
21. Ibid., p. 167.
22. Ibid., p. 173.
23. Ibid., p. 174.
24. Ibid., p. 176.
25. Ibid., p. 177.
26. Ibid., p. 184.
27. Murray, p. 23.
28. Lindsey and Carlson, pp. 29 and 71.
29. Ibid., pp. 42—44, 48, 49—50.
30. Hendriksen, p. 234.
31. Lindsey and Carlson, p. 188.

Chapter 13

1. Grier, p. 121.
2. Grier, pp. 123—124.

Chapter 14

1. Murray, p. 123.

Index of Main Bible Passages